The ABCs:
Integrating artificial, business, and competitive intelligence in the modern law firm

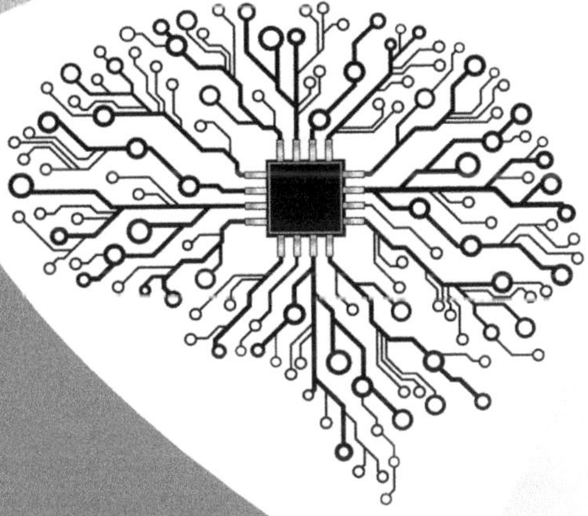

EDITED BY FRANCESCA RAMADAN

Commissioning editor
Alex Davies

Editorial assistant
Francesca Ramadan

Published by
Globe Law and Business Ltd
3 Mylor Close
Horsell
Woking
Surrey GU21 4DD
United Kingdom
Tel: +44 20 3745 4770
www.globelawandbusiness.com

ISBN: 978-1-78358-368-3
A catalogue record for this book is available from the British Library

Contents

Executive summary

The world of data, analytics, and technology is relatively unexplored in the legal arena, due to the traditionally conservative and risk-averse nature of the legal environment. However, we are approaching a reality in which data is the most precious resource of practically every single organization. Law firms should be no different. The buzz around intelligence functions and initiatives places constant emphasis on their immediate necessity; the narrative runs that firms need to invest both time and resources into their own competitive and business intelligence efforts, and complementing technologies and tools, to avoid being left behind. The fact that these disciplines are in their infancy – with their very definitions in flux and varying between different practices – does not make it any easier.

The goalposts are constantly moving, and it is common for multiple BI and CI initiatives and practices to be distributed across the breadth of the firm, from the marketing and finance departments to the library. The challenge, then, when attempting to build robust intelligence functions within a law firm, is not only to mature these efforts but also to facilitate collaboration and ensure they are centralized.

The ABCs: Integrating artificial, business, and competitive intelligence in the modern law firm acts as a practical roadmap for how to achieve exactly that, taking a deep dive into the developing disciplines of AI, BI, and CI and their potential synergies, featuring expert contributions from industry leaders covering a wide range of the most pressing issues – from how to make business development processes more systemic utilizing AI technologies, to real-world examples of competitive intelligence initiatives and their lifecycle.

One of the primary difficulties with CI and BI is that they are often conflated; workable definitions of either are hard to come by, and their relationship can frequently be ambiguous. AI, too, is often misunderstood or misnamed. In chapter one, Bernadette DeCelle – senior director of client development and marketing at McCarter & English LLP – lays the foundation for our exploration of these disciplines by providing practical characterizations of all three, before delving into their histories and outlining what firms can achieve by utilizing them in the present.

Understanding a client's propensity to buy, the likelihood of attrition, sentiment and value defense, are all analyses that organizations have been doing for years. What is new is the ability to use data to more quickly identify these risks and take action in a coordinated way. Through examining the technology "hype-cycle" and various principles learned from other industries, there are many things firms can do today to put into practice these new ideas; evidence of digital transformation in legal is mounting, with new roles such as data scientists creeping into firms to support such efforts. However, the question remains: how far along are firms and how fast do they need to act? Moreover, what new things can firms do to grapple with disruptive forces in the industry? Chapter two – by Jennifer Roberts, manager of strategic research at InTapp – explores how firms are leveraging AI, BI, and CI to expand law firm relationships with clients and address these pressing questions.

Artificial intelligence is designed to take the manual labor out of analysis, to reduce human error and compute large tracts of data. Business intelligence is the passive gathering of that data – from demographics to key strokes, frequency of use, and other repeatable quantifiable data sets. Competitive intelligence then, is the surveying of the outside world – media, market factors, and other qualitative data – and bringing it to bear; it takes into account the same analysis as AI and combines that with human intelligence, better known in today's business environment as "insight". In this study of how AI, BI, and CI need to be combined in law firms, in chapter three Zena Applebaum – director of customer insights and success at Thomson Reuters in Canada – adds human intelligence (HUMINT), or primary customer insights, into the mix – a factor unique to each firm and therefore necessarily the only true competitive advantage it can offer.

To provide proactive support that enhances profitability and drives revenue growth, the leaders of marketing and knowledge services departments and other support groups within a firm need to design effective collaboration that can coordinate their efforts throughout the business development (BD) process. In chapter four, David Kamien – CEO of Mind-Alliance Systems – delves into the leadership and process improvement approaches needed to strengthen the foundations of effective collaboration. A methodology to better organize business development processes and make them more systematic using a combination of AI technologies is also presented, along with a new paradigm for integrating intelligence into each phase of the BD process.

The idea that only the law firm of the future utilizes AI seems to be redundant; collective wisdom is insistent that firms must be incorporating it at this very moment, or risk falling behind. However, what is the real state of affairs on the ground? How are firms currently incorporating AI into their practice, and to what extent? In 2017, PP&C Consulting conducted a survey of the use of client-facing artificial intelligence in 22 leading law firms and updated their research in 2019, presented here in chapter five by Yolanda Cartusciello – partner at PP&C Consulting. This chapter provides an in-depth look at the current uses of client-facing AI, as well as insights into plans and projects for future use by these firms.

Chapter six, authored by Mark Gediman – reference librarian at Alston & Bird LLP – charts the lifecycle of a competitive intelligence function from initial pitch to workflow using actual examples. It follows the process from the crucial first steps – arguably most importantly, selling the firm on the idea of creating a dedicated group of professionals providing intelligence to support growth strategies – to the completed function, taking into account its position within the firm's hierarchy, staffing, tools, and budgeting. Emphasis is placed on another essential component of a successful competitive intelligence operation – the management of expectations. From deliverables to turnaround times, making sure that consumers of intelligence know what to expect from the competitive intelligence analysts' products increases their value; strategies to secure this, alongside attorney buy-in, are outlined.

Artificial intelligence refers to computing systems that possess advanced pattern recognition and inferential reasoning abilities. In most instances, the generalist will say that these programs perform "machine learning," which is distinguished from traditional computing based on arithmetic logic. As one might imagine, the potential for applying this technology to all sorts of data crawls is tremendous. The AI tool can be deployed in several ways involving various input methods to "teach" it recognition. Placing this firmly in the context of BI and CI analysis, in chapter seven Jeff Cohan – independent consultant and former director of knowledge management at Fitzpatrick, Cella, Harper & Scinto – explains that it is best to employ traditional taxonomy tools to classify documents, and to then use them as a template for further education. How exactly to develop this taxonomy is addressed in this chapter.

Every firm is looking to improve their capabilities around business and competitive intelligence. In order to institute change, we first must know where we are today; the challenge for most firms is the lack of framework needed to assess their current position. One can know when things are not optimized and require transformation – but what specifically do we change, and why? In chapter eight, Dave Whiteside – director of client growth and success at CLIENTSFirst – addresses these challenges through the lens of people, process, and tools, helping to identify what needs changing and which areas in the firm have assets that can be better leveraged. The most crucial question will be answered: why is the BI/CI function where it is today, and how can it be more effective?

Matter experience inside the law firm is unarguably the most informative business intelligence that should be gathered to support the sales function. Other chapters have explored how specific approaches in leadership, process improvement, and collaboration among teams can better gather this information. In the final chapter, Keith Mewe – VP of strategy and solutions at Content Pilot – discusses methods of ensuring that firms place the most applicable business intelligence – gathered matter information in perfect alignment with client need – is placed in front of potential clients, using competitive intelligence and artificial intelligence techniques to guide the way. This includes how to best use the business advantages and disadvantages of your key competitors; how a deeper understanding of the client can determine which matter experience is presented; how to determine which matter experience best resonates with clients and improves conversion rates; and how capturing nuanced business intelligence can lead to a competitive advantage.

About the authors

Zena Applebaum is director, customer insights and success at Thomson Reuters in Canada. In her role, Zena is responsible for client feedback and intelligence, market insights, and sales enablement. Prior to joining Thomson Reuters, Zena was the director of competitive intelligence at Bennett Jones LLP, having pioneered the discipline of law firm CI, and authoring *Business Intelligence for Law Firms*, published in November 2012. Zena shares her passion for the industry as a speaker, writer and contributor to blogs, including "3 Geeks and a Law Blog", with topics ranging from competitive intelligence, legal industry change management, qualitative data analysis and personal branding. A data junkie who revels in the possibilities of data to connect people, places and things, Zena can often be found connecting the dots between seemingly unrelated data. In 2015 Zena was inducted as a Fellow of the Council of CI Fellows, and she has been a sessional instructor the University of Toronto iSchool, Rutgers University and a guest lecturer at law schools across North America. She currently serves on the SLA Board of Directors.

Yolanda Cartusciello has served in senior administrative leadership roles in major law firms for more than 20 years, including Debevoise & Plimpton and Cleary Gottlieb. She has led marketing teams, designed business development and media strategies, and implemented client development programs. She has been the chief architect of profile enhancement strategies, perception studies, branding exercises, comprehensive client interview programs, and practice and lateral partner rollouts. She has adapted the customer journey mapping technique for use by law firms, and has trained and advised firms on its use. She is a frequent lecturer and author on client journey mapping and the customer experience. Yolanda has also created business development and communications training and coaching programs for lawyers at all levels.

Jeff Cohan is an independent consultant assisting with law library administration, cost efficiencies, value generation, staff utilization, information retrieval, knowledge management, competitive intelligence, business intelligence research, conflict of interest protocols, and business analytics. As a consultant, he helps firms implement procedures, practices, and technology, alongside negotiating vendor contracts. For 13 years, he was the library director and director of knowledge management at Fitzpatrick, Cella, Harper, and Scinto, an IP boutique practice based in New York; prior to that he was the library director at a regional general practice law firm. Jeff speaks regularly on topics of interest related to knowledge management, competitive intelligence, and business analytics. He sits on the board of directors for Strategic Competitive Intelligence Professionals. He is also a past president of the Law Library Association of Greater New York.

Mark Gediman is a reference librarian for Alston & Bird LLP, supporting the research needs of more than 800 attorneys and paralegals. He is a past president of the Southern California Association of Law Libraries, as well as co-founder and co-chair of the PLL-IP Competitive Intelligence Caucus. Mark writes and presents regularly on competitive intelligence, research and library management issues for the American Association of Law Libraries (AALL), Legal Marketing Association (LMA), the Special Libraries Association (SLA), SCALL, NoCALL, ACI and HALL. He has been a regular contributor to past ARK publications and has also authored articles for *AALL Spectrum*, *Practicing Law Management Week*, *Paralegal Today*, and *Facts & Findings – The Magazine of the National Association of Legal Assistants* (NALA). Mark is a graduate of the University of California – Riverside.

David Kamien is the CEO of Mind-Alliance Systems (www.mind-alliance.com). Mind-Alliance provides law firms with solutions in areas including business development research, knowledge management, and innovation. He is also the product owner of the MindPeer BD research management software system. David has supported leading clients such as Squire Patton Boggs, Ogletree Deakins, Sidley Austin, Shearman & Sterling, and Saul Ewing. He is the editor of the seminal McGraw-Hill *Homeland Security Handbook* (2005, 2012 editions) and the inventor of a patented method for improving organizational information sharing and collaboration. David holds a law degree from the Academic College of Law and a BA from Hebrew University.

Jennifer Roberts manages the strategic research function at Intapp, responsible for the analytics and research component that supports product development and thought leadership for new initiatives. Leveraging her skills to advocate, evangelize and build data-fueled products and insight, she examines the professional services industry to drive analytical intelligence that informs strategic decisions and solves organizational needs. Prior to joining Intapp, Jennifer received her MA from the University of Minnesota in advanced statistical methodology and performance measures.

Keith Wewe is the VP of strategy and solutions at Content Pilot, a marketing, technology and business development consultancy for law firms, and former international president of the Legal Marketing Association. One of the many aspects of his work is to connect the dots for clients between the receipt of proposal/RFP and the ultimate win. To achieve that, he works with large firms to regional boutiques creating laser-focused proposal content, business intelligence, template designs, go/no-go plans, response strategies, win/loss debriefs and analytics research that help them create better proposals that align with client needs with the goal of achieving that win. You can follow him on Twitter at @kwewe and Linked In at www.linkedin.com/in/keithwewe.

Dave Whiteside is director of client growth & success at CLIENTSFirst. Dave's focus is helping the company grow and expand its CRM, data quality, eMarketing and client intelligence service offerings, and building alliances that help deliver additional value to clients. With more than 30 years of sales and marketing experience, Dave offers clients extensive knowledge of marketing technology and business development in legal, accounting and professional services business environments. Known primarily for his deep knowledge of business development processes and technologies such as CRM and competitive intelligence, Dave is well-respected for the high level of service he provides his clients who call on him regularly for advice.

Prior to joining CLIENTSFirst, Dave held numerous sales and sales management roles at Thomson Reuters, in the legal and accounting marketing technology software and services areas. Previously, Dave was vice president of a project management software and services organization, managing the sales and professional services teams while developing project management expertise. Dave is a well-known speaker in the legal marketing industry and actively participates in the

Legal Marketing Association (LMA). A graduate of Lake Superior State University with a degree in Marketing, Dave also holds a MBA from St Mary's College in California.

Chapter 1: Knowing your ABCs – defining the intelligence functions

By Bernadette DeCelle, senior director of client development and marketing at McCarter & English LLP

Artificial intelligence, business intelligence, and competitive intelligence are terms heard frequently in law firms these days. This chapter sets the stage for the book, briefly defining and providing a bit of history on each term. While the terms have been used for decades, this book's goal is to focus on the rapid advancements of artificial intelligence in the past decade and how those improvements have broadened the business intelligence offerings, which, in turn, have expanded the competitive intelligence available to all law firms. Whether you are in a large firm or are a sole practitioner, there are numerous intelligence tools available in the legal marketplace to improve your competitive advantage. We will also explain the inter-relationship of the ABCs of intelligence and how they are changing the legal landscape.

It begins with A...

Artificial intelligence (AI) was a term coined in the 1950s by a group of scientists attending a conference at Dartmouth to mean intelligence demonstrated by machines. While computers of that era could execute complex commands, they were not capable of storing those commands. Computers lacked the memory to remember previous actions and could not "learn" from previous commands to make informed decisions and solve future problems. At the Dartmouth conference, three researchers funded by the RAND Corporation presented the Logic Theorist, which was a computer program developed to mimic the problem-solving skills of a human brain. The program generated great enthusiasm, providing a roadmap for AI, creating software that took several more decades to become a functioning reality.

Voice recognition software exemplifies the complexities and challenges of developing artificial intelligence applications. The programs that drive many of the digital assistants that have become ubiquitous in the last decade, from companies such as Google, Amazon, Apple and Microsoft, have taken over 50 years to develop. Voice recognition applications were the goal of many of the scientists attending the conference at Dartmouth, but the enormous amounts of programming and computing power needed to "teach" the computer how to recognize each word in the English language, and understand its syntax and variations, took decades to fine-tune.

A brief history of the development of voice recognition software helps explain how artificial intelligence has progressed. In 1952, Bell Labs developed a system that recognized the ten individual numbers spoken by a human voice. Ten years later, in 1962, the technology had advanced to recognize 16 spoken English words. In the 1970s, Carnegie Mellon's system could understand 1,011 words – the equivalent of a three-year old's vocabulary. The 1970s to the 1980s saw big advancements due to US government funding of the research. Systems now recognized about 5,000 words, because the machines were being taught to "think" by using a new statistical method that incorporated the probability of sounds being words. As processing power improved in the 80s and 90s, computer systems advanced to understand the variations in speech patterns, and words, producing commercial applications such as voice-activated typing programs and voice-activated telephone menus. Voice recognition software has continually progressed to now think like our brains, using logic to understand syntax, accents, and recognize the difference between homophones (cell vs sell). It has also expanded to understand hundreds of languages and dialects.

Today's voice recognition systems have continually advanced from previous generations' applications, through artificial intelligence, from early programs where the computer recognized a sound pattern to equal one specific word, to machine-learning models – where the computer is taught to recognize key words and use predictive analytics to interpret what was said. Google's Voice Search now has 230 billion words incorporated into its algorithms, continually improving by learning from real-life queries of its users. AI has helped Google increase the accuracy of its voice recognition from 77 percent in 2013 to 95 percent in 2017, which is now the equivalent of a human being. To put that in perspective, it took scientists ten years in the 1950s to have a computer recognize 16 words. Through AI applications, Google's software has improved the number of words it recognizes by 40 billion words in only four short years. The software has finally improved enough to think like the human brain, while scientists have been working on the problem for over 67 years.

In the legal industry, many of the first applications to use artificial intelligence were in the e-discovery arena. In the late 90s, software applications would analyze thousands of pages of documents and electronic files (emails, documents and metadata), identifying which pages contained key words relevant to a case. As machine-learning applications have evolved they have improved the identification of key words to eliminate false positives and markedly increase the accuracy of the results. Today, e-discovery software has evolved to not just highlight key words, but to also use predictive coding and machine-learning principles, to identify the most relevant documents in a case. The software looks at the other words surrounding the key word and extrapolates the context to more accurately identify relevant documents. By significantly reducing the number of documents for human review, the software enables great savings to companies, during the discovery process in litigation.

Another use of artificial intelligence applications that is gaining traction in law firms is the use of automation tools that allow their clients to create the initial forms and contracts on their own, saving valuable time and money. Whether the system drafts the documents needed for a company to incorporate or the initial forms for a patent, much of the process can be handled by an AI system and later reviewed by a lawyer.

It moves onto B...

Business intelligence is usually defined as the tools, processes, and software applications that an organization uses to convert either internal or industry data into actionable business decisions. There are numerous business intelligence applications that use artificial intelligence to improve the efficiency of a legal organization, which will be explored below.

The term has a long history, first used in a book published in 1865, by Richard Millar Devens. He used the term to describe a banker whose network of informants provided the banker with the outcomes of battles being won or lost across Northern Europe. That information enabled the banker to gain advantages over his competitors. The term was updated in the late 1950s, by IBM researchers to include computer-aided models that were employed to assist in decision-making and planning. Circling back to our artificial intelligence discussion above, IBM was one of the companies to recognize the value of voice recognition software, using it to develop real-world applications including voice-activated typewriters and computers and creating efficiencies for their customers. Fast forward to today, leading companies also use their voice recognition applications as business intelligence tools – Google being a prime example of an application that millions use globally. Whether the request is spoken or typed, Google's systems capture every search request to improve its base of knowledge. Algorithms then use that knowledge base to organize and improve all future search results provided by Google's applications. Upon the next similar request, Google is also then able to present sponsored ads that are more relevant to the requestor, in addition to capturing other data (location, demographics, etc.) that may be of value to their advertisers.

In the legal industry, business intelligence tools cover just about every aspect of a company's operations, from finance, human resources and knowledge management to business development and marketing. Tools include those that collect and analyze data from disparate sources and databases to feed into web-based dashboards where the information is designed in an easy way to allow the user to make actionable business decisions based on the data. The impressive business intelligence tools available today utilize machine-learning and artificial intelligence to offer law firms a wealth of information.

Law firms are able to use a multitude of business intelligence tools to help in all areas of their practice, from billing and pricing to business development. Consider, for example, the databases that capture the outcomes of court cases and allow users to search a number of criteria – including how a judge rules, how long it takes and the types of legal issues covered – that enable lawyers to advise their client on whether and/or how a case should proceed. Another example is the "listening platform", an aggregator that scrapes the web every time a desired search term shows up in the news and social media (sifting out the duplicate articles and near misses). Companies and law firms can greatly benefit from this process, staying on top of a client or competitor quickly and efficiently.

It ends with C

This leads us full circle to competitive intelligence. There are many definitions of competitive intelligence, due to variances of how different industries use it. It is essentially the art of analyzing the mountain of information – produced by the business intelligence and artificial intelligence applications – to create actionable insights about the marketplace and/or specific competitors that enable one to develop a plan of action to gain a competitive advantage. While people have been utilizing various forms of competitive intelligence much earlier than the 1980s, the term came into popular use at that time with the creation of the Society of Competitive Intelligence Professionals in 1985.

The 1980s were also when larger law firms were beginning to build internal marketing and business development departments. The legal marketing professionals within those firms began applying the same principles of competitive intelligence (CI) in their law firm roles, as they had in the industries from which they came. As the internet was not available to businesses, the pool of data was much smaller – annual reports and quarterly filings, news clipping services that often lagged far behind, and legal databases that consisted of dial-up services using dedicated terminals. Eventually law firms realized that there were valuable insights to be gained by using the same industry databases that their clients did, and savvy firms invested in those same tools.

The sophistication and amount of CI tools available today is overwhelming, which is why many firms have dedicated CI professionals to evaluate the wide array of tools available for their organization, and to provide streamlined data analysis for better decision-making. This is covered more fully in chapter six, detailing how firms are structuring their teams to improve their bottom line.

Firms use CI to add data-based insights when making decisions in any number of areas, including:

- **Strategic planning**: what industries and practices should be promoted; determining if there is upside potential to a merger or whether an office should be opened in a new region;
- **News aggregators**: to identify market trends and benchmark competitors and to stay on top of clients' information;
- **Pricing**: identifying competitor rates, client buying history, pricing of alternative fee arrangements, matter budgeting, among other issues; and
- **Client feedback programs**: automated web surveys, portals and other tools to help firms continue to "listen" to their clients.

When a law firm gains key insights into how and where competitors operate – how they price their services, what types of clients and cases they take on – they are able to competitively market their services to be more appealing to the prospective client. Competitive intelligence can also allow a firm to address challenges they may have in the delivery of services, improving client service and gaining further traction in their relationship with the client.

As an example, a firm can synch their client's data with a commercial system that tracks the court filings of those clients. Utilizing a developer's short script to match the client data in both databases, the computer can alert the competitive intelligence team when the system identifies that a firm's client has been named in a lawsuit. If after the CI team analyzes the information and decides the firm has the legal expertise needed to defend the lawsuit, they can present the opportunity to the relationship lawyer. Utilizing other research tools on the market, the CI team can also provide the relationship lawyer with a summary of what other law firms represent the same client; the success of those firms in previous cases; if the judge or the jurisdiction may present hurdles; and other information that the relationship lawyer can easily assess as to whether there is a possibility to pursue that piece of business. In addition, the lawyer can summarize the firm's expertise and advantages, to persuade the client that they are the right firm to handle the case. Connecting the case information into the firm's financial software and pricing tools, the CI team or pricing team can also evaluate whether it would be profitable to take that type of work on.

As the above example demonstrates, this scenario required the ability of internal and external databases to speak to each other, and for a CI professional and relationship lawyer to analyze the data and act on it. With a bit of development time to integrate these internal and external databases, your firm can create some very powerful tools to deliver the intelligence the CI team needs to present a strategic analysis to the relationship lawyer. That data would be the basis for drafting a persuasive proposal to the client for the opportunity to represent them.

Looping back to the abilities of artificial intelligence (AI), eventually there will be systems that learn from past results to improve the information it sends to users, optimizing the data output to only send lawsuits filed that the firm has a chance of actually succeeding in winning the engagement.

While that day is not here yet, it will be here sooner than we expect. As the voice recognition software discussion above demonstrated, software has improved in the last decade at a far greater rate than the previous six decades combined. The competitive intelligence tools are rapidly evolving to enable law firms to make more data-informed decisions quickly, identifying opportunities and risks and providing those firms that embrace the technology with a strong advantage over those that do not.

Chapter 2:

Law firm modernization – leveraging intelligence to transform relationships

By Jennifer Roberts, manager of strategic research at InTapp

Over the last decade since the demand for legal services plummeted, law firms have had to find new and creative ways to remain relevant. In the early innings of the demand decline, the gut reaction of many firms was to cut costs (Figure 1), dipping the lowest in 2010 when the industry saw massive cuts across the lawyer pool in Big Law. However, this only got firms so far; while partner profits stabilized as the denominator shrunk and expenses leveled out, new entrants quickly moved into the market, clients gained the upper hand, and a dichotomy took root, dividing top-performing firms and those that fell behind. With the exponential growth of lateral moves and continued consolidation of firms, there is no slowing in the changes firms need to make to differentiate and compete.

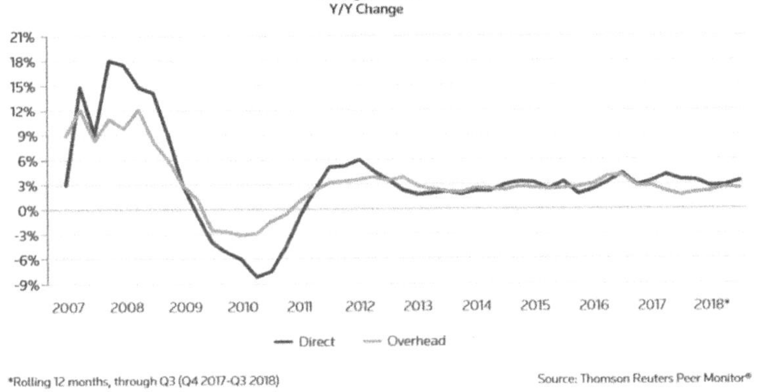

Figure 1: Expense growth. Source: Thomson Reuters Peer Monitor

Georgetown, Altman Weil, Citi Group and others studying the market reveal that, with the intensified competition, cutting costs and changes triggering mediocre revenue growth will no longer cut it. Firms have to change not only the way they practice law but also the way they deal with the business of law, the latter being a mandatory focus in order to differentiate and win.

It comes down to enabling an operating model to support the effort. A recent McKinsey study on bold innovation shows that financially successful enterprises outperform their peers by employing newer types of operating models that require a more systematic and rapid approach. The study shows that winners have taken on larger risks and placed bolder bets – phenomena not natural to most law firms, as lawyers remain risk-averse.

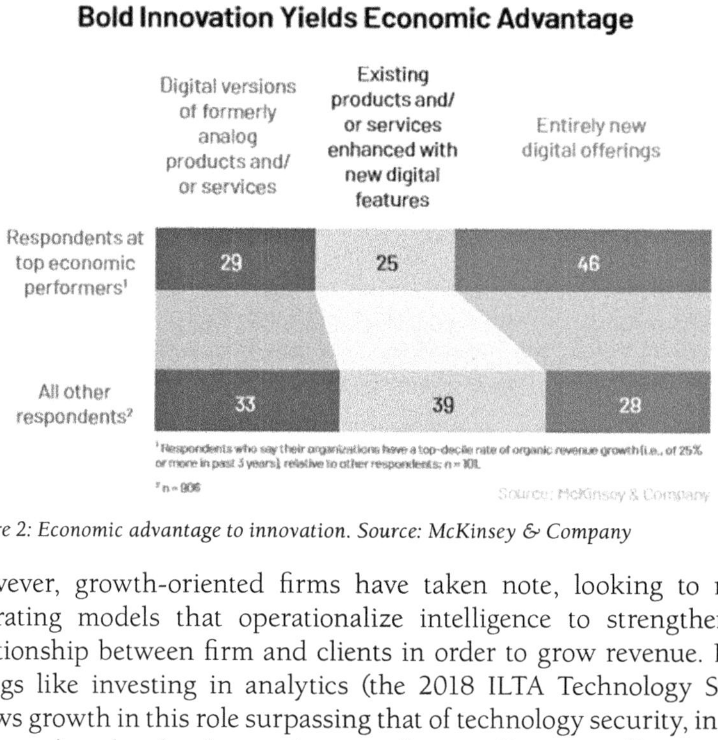

Figure 2: Economic advantage to innovation. Source: McKinsey & Company

However, growth-oriented firms have taken note, looking to newer operating models that operationalize intelligence to strengthen the relationship between firm and clients in order to grow revenue. Doing things like investing in analytics (the 2018 ILTA Technology Survey shows growth in this role surpassing that of technology security, in some instances) and technology to leverage firm intelligence will expand the relationship with clients. After all, according to the Calibrate and Intapp 2018 Growth Enablement Survey, additional business from existing clients is the single best source of business for nearly 80 percent of firms (figure 2). Luckily, what firms need to retain and growth these clients is already within the firm – that is, intelligence about the client, their industry, what services they buy, what services they need (before they even know), and how it all aligns with firm strategy. It comes down to how a firm leverages this intelligence that sets them apart.

Figure 3: Best source of firm business. Source: 2018 Law Firm Growth Enablement Survey

Firm intelligence

Beyond the lawyer, a major asset of a firm is intelligence. Specifically, there are treasure troves of data waiting to be turned into firm intelligence from financial management systems, document management systems, experience solutions, CRMs and intake systems. These are just a few primary sources; there are third-party sources as well, such as Dunn and Bradstreet – which are used during conflicts checks and in research and library services but have yet to be tapped by the broader firm – that can bolster the intelligence a firm has on the client. Despite having all this data, it's been difficult to leverage due to disparate systems, issues of dirty data, lack of collaboration, and the shortage of a data culture at the firm. That aside, firms have used this information on an ad-hoc basis, manually bringing it together to undergo performance tracking and inform market opportunities such as practice expansion. Thinking about the data and use cases currently at law firms, it can be boiled down to:

1. **Business intelligence (BI)** – offers historical, current, and future perspectives of business operations. BI responsibilities include querying, reporting, triggering and alerts to bring business analytics to real-time. BI is best produced when internal data from financial and operations are combined with external market data to help put things into perspective. Currently used at the firm for functions such as finance, business development, and pricing; and
2. **Competitive intelligence (CI)** – offers the external market data needed to add context to business intelligence. CI involves gathering, analyzing and disseminating information typically focused on the market and firms' competitors. Primarily leveraged in business development and research currently at the firm.

BI and CI play well together, offering a nice holistic story to answer the pertinent questions firms need insight on to win in the current market. However, the efforts have been rather lackluster when compared to other industries outside of legal, as these analyses prove to be arduous, ad-hoc and manual. Additionally, the lack of trust in data and lawyers' predisposition to skepticism has put a lot of the progress in how a firm may operationalize this intelligence on the back burner. However, with market pressure and the evolving technologies in artificial intelligence (AI), legal can take note from other industries to bring the abundance of firm data, systematize and operationalize it in new ways to amplify the intelligence available to the firm.

AI is defined as the intelligence demonstrated by a machine; when a machine mimics the cognitive functions of a human, such as learning and problem-solving, it is then considered AI.[1] When it comes to AI and operationalizing intelligence, there is plenty to be learned from other industries. For example, law firms should not get so hung up on issues of dirty data; in fact, data janitorial activities take up between 50-80 percent of most data scientist resources[2] across all industries. Because of this, there are many tools and techniques out there to fill in missing data, remove extraneous data, provide structure, and derive new data points in order to secure a robust data set to extract meaningful insights. Chatbots, voice assistants, predictive text and prescriptive analytics have shown notable improvements for health outcomes, client retention and cross-selling in healthcare, retail, and accounting. While the use cases might be different, the principle remains: AI can be leveraged to bring intelligence forward at the fingertips of the provider (i.e. the lawyer) and enhance the relationship between organization and client.

The AI market has recognized the opportunity in legal. Legal technology start-ups have become the rage, focusing on data-centric applications and AI. In 2018 alone, they have raised over $1 billion in funding, with over a third of that focused on AI and the use of data.[3] The potential of AI in legal enables firms to automate and operationalize firm intelligence, bringing data together to proliferate BI and CI, rendering it proactive and the center of operations (if they are willing to engrain the data culture into the fabric of the firm). In the end, the potential of AI offers a wide-range tool that empowers firms to rethink how they integrate information, analyze data, and utilize the results.

When thinking about AI in legal and assessing the technology that is emerging, it is important to take a step back and assess the emerging technology against the backdrop of Gartner's hype cycle. The market climate outlined above certainly acts as a stimulating event to spur innovation as firms scramble to differentiate. The period of "innovation trigger" is just behind us; the proliferation of technology and the promises, the early wins as well as losses, suggests the industry is somewhere between "peak of inflated expectations" and "trough of disillusionment", depending on the application of technology. That isn't to deter excitement around what AI has to offer; however, remain realistic as firms work to configure the best use to drive growth.

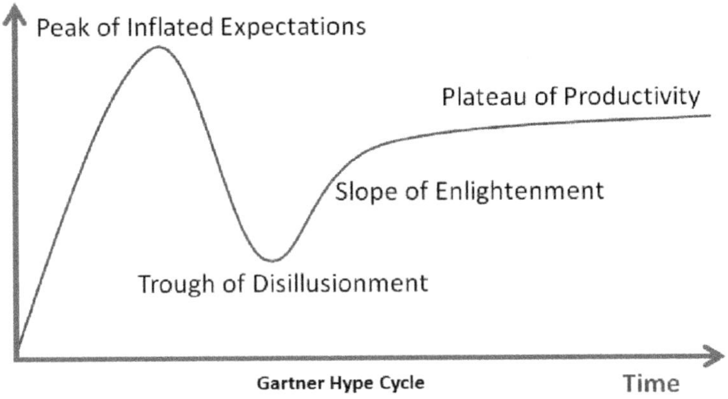

Figure 4: Technology hype cycle. Source: Gartner

The key to the hype cycle when applying AI at the firm is ensuring the reduction of risk in investment decisions. That being said, it is important to understand the business value that the technology can provide in the context of the firm. While not easy, this is something that innovative firms have accomplished in its early innings to get at quick wins.

Evidence of innovation: introducing the data scientist

In considering the operationalization of intelligence at the firm, the market is showing signs – albeit small – of pointing in the right direction. Specifically, as firms move further away from analog, creating more and more data, there then comes the need for leveraging that data. Data science is the next step in the progression to get a better understanding of the use cases available, coupled with AI to consume the data, derive intelligence, and create value in an automated fashion. To this end, along with the rising spend within firm in technology, roles geared towards the advancement of analytics are cropping up at firms. Titles like chief data scientist, chief value officer, chief analytics officer and chief innovation officer are signs of the advancement in maturity.

The proliferation of these titles implies recognition at the firm regarding the need to bring firm intelligence forward in order to differentiate in the market; however, even more importantly, there is a recognition of the assets that the firm can leverage to get them there, specifically data. As noted, firms have a lot of it. The analysis of this asset isn't new to the firm. Analytics roles have been at firms for decades; as noted, the focus has mainly been on reactive competitive and business intelligence, commonly with a financial heritage and mainly on the descriptive and diagnostics questions posed by firms. Analysts typically come from varying backgrounds and often pull static reports that provide insight into costs, financial performance, and market opportunity. Frequently, they are the leaders in data visualization and storytelling with data. If it were not for the efforts of these professionals through the years, the opportunity for the data scientist might be quite limited. The traditional analyst has set the foundation for the data age, as the vision of the data-driven firm builds on these efforts.

The role of the data scientist within law firms is new but rapidly developing. According to a recent study on the rise of the legal data scientist by Intapp and Law Vision, which asked 65 firm executives about innovation and investment in analytics, one-third of the firms in the survey have at least one data scientist (most have two), with most hired in the last two years. An additional 12 percent plan to hire a data scientist over the next year, further establishing a foothold for the role.

In terms of responsibilities, in contrast to the analyst, the data scientist typically possesses a blend of formal analytical skills in statistics, joined by computer science, a depth of knowledge in databases and software, as well as data visualization and storytelling skills. Senior data scientists are likely to possess an executive skill set and an understanding of what data means to the business, as well as an ability to put it to use. They are leveraged within the firm to help operationalize analytics, creating feedback and learning to become more proactive and real-time, as well as deal with many of the data issues firms typically use as a barrier to the establishment of a data culture. As the use cases grow and the role gains more presence in legal, further refinement will occur in terms of value add. However, there are notable wins for earlier movers.

Against the backdrop of 2018 performance, we see a common theme: better performing firms consistently make larger investments in innovative projects and client development. Specifically, of the firms that responded to this survey with positive revenue growth in 2018, more than half employed a data scientist or plan to do so within the next 12 months. Conversely, no firms with neutral or negative revenue growth in 2018 currently employ data scientists, and only 33 percent plan to hire one in the next 12 months.

How far are firms, really?

The more data a firm has and the more frequently it is used, the more valuable the intelligence becomes, as functions become reliant on the insight and a benchmark is established for analytics' success in an organization. Gartner's data model, visually illustrated below, classifies data into four zones: descriptive statistics, which focus on what happened; diagnostic, which describe why it happened; predictive, which forecast what will happen; and prescriptive, which provide guidelines for what to do about it.

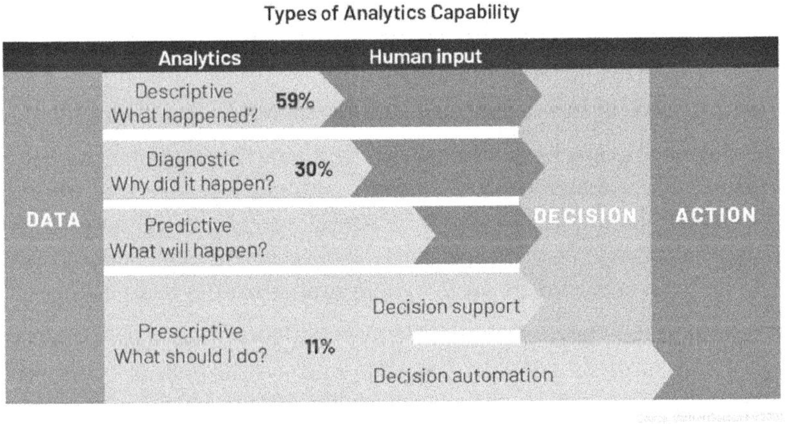

Figure 5: Analytics maturity model. Source: Gartner & 2019 Rise of the legal data scientist survey

The primary data uses at the firm – according to the Intapp and Law Vision Rise of the Legal Data Scientist study against the backdrop of the Gartner analytics model – confirmed that the majority (59 percent) are mostly performing descriptive analyses. Another 30 percent claim to be playing in the diagnostic category; surprisingly, 11 percent of the respondents leapt two steps into prescriptive analytics. The model emphasizes that prescriptive equals a highly automated intelligent guidance system. The respondents in the prescriptive group, in fact, are operating prescriptively, but are relying more on human labor than the model is allowing.

In terms of the application of analytics, as highlighted by the Gartner model, it is still in the initial stages, which is only emphasized when looking at the applications of analytics. Over 70 percent of firms are only using analytics and data science applications predominantly for internal solutions – functions that address pricing, profitability, and firm configuration. While internal applications are surely critical for firm success, there remains even more potential for firms to venture externally and understand the application of data science towards improving the relationship between firm and client, which will have a stronger impact on business model improvement. Opportunities that leverage the firm's intelligence to bolster the relationship between client and firm include:

- **Cross-selling** – prediction about buying and guidance about next steps to take. This is based off clients that look similar from a data perspective and something frequently done in other industries based on propensity to buy, buyer behavior and buying bundles. Client intelligence of this magnitude empowers business development;
- **Relationship strength** – measuring depth and breadth of relationships to aid in understanding the health and relative risk of attribution. Bringing data together from financial management systems and experience management solutions to convey client intelligence forward to help lawyers identify areas to help strengthen the relationship;
- **Client risk** – beyond just clearing conflicts, clients can also bring with them other risk like bad debt or even the risk of bringing in the wrong work with misalignment between the firm's strategy and the type of work a client wants to bring to a firm. Operationalizing client data transforms the intake process in order to enable intelligent decisions from the beginning during client intake; and
- **Legal project management** – outside of just tracking in spreadsheets and guesstimates, higher level analytics and AI can take project management to the next level. Providing real data on actuals vs budgets, automated tracking and predictive resourcing in order to bring the best talent forward. This intelligence provides firms a leg up to the competition by offering transparency as well as increased partner per profit contribution at the matter level.

There is still a way to go in terms of the application of analytics in legal; despite the investment in bringing data scientist into the fold, there still seems to be a disconnect. In order to realize higher value, there must be investment and commitment to the role as well as a connection to firm strategy. Respondents to the Rise of the Legal Analyst study were asked about the usefulness of analytics; unsurprisingly, over 80 percent of the respondents indicated this function was useful, suggesting an appreciation for the importance of data. However, only 53 percent have incorporated data and analytics into the firm's strategy. There exists a clear misalignment between usefulness and value for the 27 percent of firms that find it useful but don't incorporate it into strategy, and for those that don't even find it useful at all.

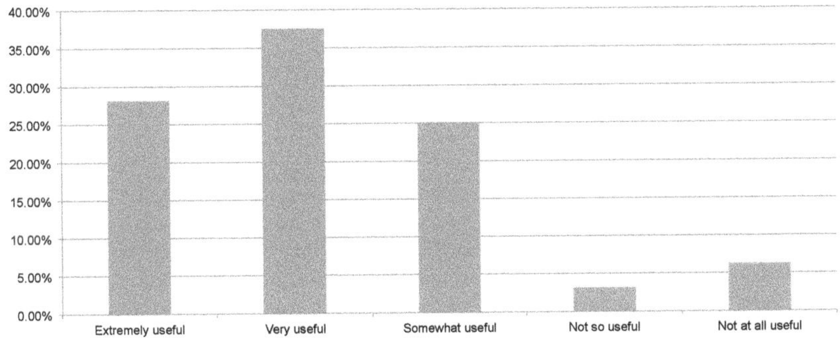

Figure 6: Usefulness of analytics at law firms. Source: 2019 Rise of the legal data scientist survey

Furthermore, aligning these results against 2018 performance, only 30 percent of neutral or negative growth firms use data analytics as a part of their strategies, and only a very small proportion recognize it as useful. This poses a stark contrast to those firms with positive growth, where 56 percent incorporate data analytics into firm-wide strategy and a majority identify data and analytics as extremely useful.

What's next?

Beyond the investment in technology and expanding roles for analytics, firms must align value and strategy to truly operationalize intelligence. Moreover, the adoption of analytics and data science into the firm is a step forward, as the data science practice can help materialize the potential and open the door for things like AI and automation on a large scale. This includes supervised machine learning, which only improves the data and insight available to the firm. AI also opens the door to freeing up time in tasks that are currently time consuming like analyses into business insights and data capture. Once automated, professionals now have time for higher value work.

As seen in other industries once intelligence is turned into action, the results equate to revenue and savings – reason enough for law firms to take another look at re-engineering the firm's operating model to include the operationalization of its intelligence. As more firms bring this into the fold, it will rapidly develop into a critical part of firm success. Specifically, when firms treat data as an asset to fuel their intelligence and hire data scientists to maximize its value, they can make bolder – and better informed – bets on innovative projects and client development that transform the business model. As new technologies and market changes increase competitive pressure, adopting a forward-looking, data-as-an-asset strategy will not be optional. Operationalizing intelligence will be the DNA that brings major firm stakeholders together for improved collaboration, systematic work stream improvements, and increased profitability.

References

1. Russell, Stuart J.; Norvig, Peter (2009). *Artificial Intelligence: A Modern Approach* (3rd ed.). Upper Saddle River, New Jersey: Prentice Hall. ISBN 978-0-13-604259-4.
2. https://www.nytimes.com/2014/08/18/technology/for-big-data-scientists-hurdle-to-insights-is-janitor-work.html
3. https://blog.lawgeex.com/legaltech-hits-1-billion-investment-as-lawyers-embrace-automation/

Chapter 3:
Data doesn't make decisions – the case for HUMINT in a world of AI, BI, and CI

By Zena Applebaum, director of customer insights and success at Thomson Reuters, Canada

"It's not what you know, but who you know" is an old adage of the business world. The adage maxim suggests that hard skills, knowledge and training are irrelevant next to keeping the "right" company; the boss who can promote you, the friend who is "Linked In" to several hundred others in an industry you wish to enter, or the travel agent you know from the coffee shop who can get you a deal on your next vacation. There is doubt that who you know is important; being connected to others is what makes us human. In recent years, with the explosion of technology, it has become much easier for people to connect and interact over shared interests, hobbies, and politics.

While technology-mediated connections have grown with the advent of social media, law firms too have jumped on this opportunity by creating user groups, practice/interest microsites, and alumni collaboration tools. Law firms, known for being a long-standing relationship business, have also almost rejected social media and increased the frequency of in-person events – from golf tournaments to intimate roundtable discussions, and high-impact gala events.

However we choose to interact, there is no getting away from the connectivity and importance of relationships and who you know driving your business. By that logic, who you know is important, but more important is knowing what to do with that connection. How do you harness your connectivity for the sake of your business? What value is there in your relationships – if any – beyond the fulfillment of the basic human need to connect? The question of relationship value has long been studied and is the basis of CRM systems and databases across enterprises. Recently, however, the effect of personal connections has been overshadowed by algorithms (or "algos" in the industry press) as the leading indicator of a company's competitive position and related success. There have been countless articles, papers, speeches, and panel discussions at various conferences and publications which look to define the power of artificial intelligence to transform the legal industry – from better e-discovery, to increasing firm financial acumen and pricing applications, to associate utilization and other file management techniques. In some respects, to effectively harness AI, we must reduce relationships, which are complex emotional connections, into binary static data.

Artificial intelligence is designed to take the manual labour out of analysis, to reduce human error, and identify patterns in large amounts of data faster than humans using business intelligence passively gathered based on demographic data, key strokes, time and billing information, and other repeatable quantifiable data sets. Artificial intelligence is not artificial; it is based on real data that has been created or exists by way of a series of quantifiable absolutes. Think of intelligence in this scenario as the operator in the equation – it is the analysis you apply to make sense of assumptions based on the data and then using those assumptions to predict future outcomes based on a series of repeatable absolutes.

An example would be that if every time you meet with Fred, he orders a tea, the statistical likelihood of him ordering a coffee is reduced to almost nothing. Computers can collect and analyze this data faster and better than humans ever can. For example, computers can track Fred's beverage orders everyday at any location, rather your ability to only track what he drinks when he is with you. AI can *and will* change law firm operations and business development, and even the practice of law as it relates to repeatable actions.

For example, we can apply AI to measure the time it takes to do "typical" due diligence and charge accordingly for it, or we can apply AI algorithms to pricing that M&A transaction based on similar experience; furthermore, AI can provide detail around which pieces and parts of a typical M&A should be assigned a flat fee vs those that should be priced in a bespoke manner. Moreover, by comparing your firm's internal data to that of the industry, AI can also show you how your rates or phasing of the transactions compare to industry standards, and to the client expectations and objectives. Client expectations is where the human element – the relationships, the HUMINT or human intelligence – comes into play.

Like word processing, AI is here to stay – it's the technology underpinning much of what exists or will exist in the background, supporting law firms and legal departments. If used correctly, it should only be talked about by those programming it. On a daily basis, we need to be aware of its presence and capabilities, and we need to be respectful of how we input data to make the best use of AI; however, more importantly, we need to learn to live in the world where it is as common as Wi-Fi and streaming media. We need to adapt our work process, workflows and our life habits to it, but don't need to understand its intricacies. AI is a *what* we know, not a *who*. If we believe the old adage, we really should be looking at the "whos" of our business world and how we can apply intelligence to the *who*, to make better, more informed, smarter decisions.

Who we know is the people, not the data, that surrounds our business decisions. Those people can be colleagues, clients, partners, suppliers, consumers – their similarities can only be matched by their difference in terms of their demographic, socioeconomic, geographic or industrial classification, or other quantifiable data. In the course of a typical work day, we come into contact with all kinds of people and with all kinds of opinions. Opinions are not repeatable and are informed by years of bias, training, social and economic factors, education and unique individual experience. Emotions and the ability to understand context and their impact on business is not something we can apply AI towards yet. And so, we look to CI to help us understand the "who" of our legal worlds and how *who* we know impacts us more than *what* we know in the context of the legal industry.

Competitive intelligence as a discipline takes the outside world of non-binary objects such as media, market fluctuation and demands, social agenda and interests, as well as other qualitative data, and bringing those to bear in relation to the people who create them. Competitive intelligence uses similar analysis techniques and frameworks as AI, but limited by human capabilities rather than computational analysis, and it takes into consideration human intelligence or HUMINT, as mentioned earlier – also known as the "who we know" and what they have told us, to help businesses like law firms make decisions, avoid surprises, and plan for the future. Competitive intelligence has been practiced in industry since the early 80s at companies like Motorola and Kodak.

The discipline has waivered over the years, fighting for a seat at the proverbial management table, whether reporting in through R&D, strategy, marketing, finance or sales. Recently, I think CI has come into its own, with many rebranding or repositioning traditional competitive intelligence as "competitive" or "consumer insights" or, in the case of law firms, "client insights". This rebrand is significant, as it removes the absolute nature of intelligence – such as we see with AI – and replaces it with something more human-centered.

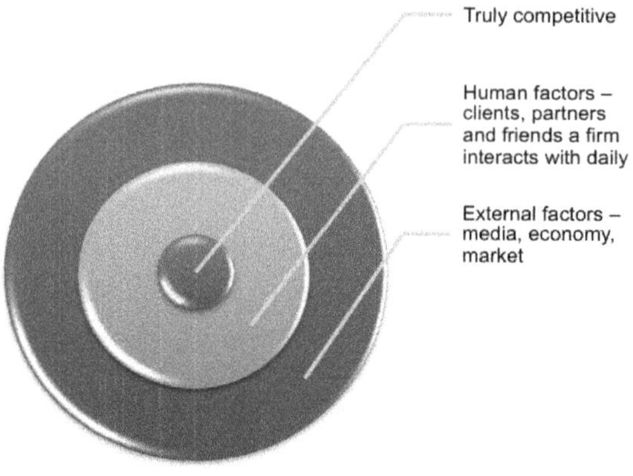

Figure 1: Epicentre of competition

Insights, as defined by the *Merriam Webster Dictionary*, is:

1. The power or act of seeing into a situation, penetration; and
2. The act or result of apprehending the inner nature of things or of seeing intuitively.

To see intuitively is to talk to people and understand what is happening and the context behind an action. "Insights" has positive connotations, and relates to a human-centred interaction rather than intelligence, which tends to be issue-focused. When you think of insights, you conjure images of Archimedes in the bathtub screaming "Eureka!", or Sherlock and Watson solving a great mystery using the facts they know and the pieces they have been able to deduce based on conversations as well as what they know from the context of the situation.

For years in my classrooms and across seminars I have suggested that HUMINT – the combination of customer primary research and elicitation – when paired with analyzed external market data is the only true competitive advantages that firms have. It is the characteristic that keeps each firm unique and successful, as detailed in Figure 1.

HUMINT in action

To understand the power of HUMINT to transform intelligence into insights, let's look at a couple of typical law firm examples.

Firm A knows it needs to grow its book of business to compete and has a couple of clients in a city in which they don't already have an office.

A partner suggests that a way to grow would be to invest in that city and open an office. Typically, research here would begin with assessing the market for work in the city, reading government reports, looking at census and regional economic data, assessing other law firms and their clients in the area, reading local papers, looking at Twitter and LinkedIn accounts for the city, and so on. Typically, one would talk to Firm A attorneys who currently work on the files for the clients who are based in the city. Additionally, one should talk to the clients in that city themselves to gauge their interest in having Firm A open an office in their home city, as well as reaching out to prospects, partner business and others in the region. The talk track, survey questions and elicitation techniques a firm uses to have these conversations should be wholly unique to Firm A and its strategic priority at the moment. All of the collected unstructured and secondary data would be categorized and analyzed using a framework or two of choice (Porter's Five Forces, Scenario Planning, PESTLE, for example), and then a course of action would be recommended. The critical piece here is that any law firm looking to open in the same city could do the same secondary research, and would mostly likely have access to the same facts. For the most part there is information parity when it comes to secondary research, and the internet and social media make this even more apparent. The unique elements of this analysis come from the HUMINT, as no two firms are going to interview the same list of people with the same questions and the same intention. To than end, the HUMINT and what insights (information and context) one can gather will make a Firm A's decision to open (or not) in the city truly unique to the competitive position of that firm and will in turn be a key driver of the decision's success rate.

In another example, Firm A is responding to an RFP from a prospect along with six competitors. In addition to answering the RFP questions as required and doing the typical CI supporting research of determining the likelihood of winning (AI can support here too with the right data!) by reviewing the incumbent firm, understanding the mission, vision and situation of the prospect, Firm A is well-positioned to win. But what if the firm took it a step further, using HUMINT to interview clients of the prospect, users of the product or service of the RFP issuing company, or talking to others known to the prospect? By distilling this HUMINT and incorporating it in to the RFP response, Firm A will demonstrate that it knows and understands the business needs of the prospect in a different way than any other firm bidding. Again, no two firms are going to ask the same questions to the same people in the same way. How Firm

A chooses to use that information in its RFP response will demonstrate its truly unique competitive edge. HUMINT and the insights gathered from those interactions is the bullseye of competitive advantage.

Harnessing who you know

If we have established that who you know is more important than what you know, as per the two examples above, what can firms do to harness who they know?

1. **Encourage the sharing of firm contacts** in a CRM database. The sharing of contacts is not about stealing clients or origination credit. Sharing contacts allows a firm to harness its best competitive weapon – relationships – for the benefit of the entire firm. It is only by knowing who you know that you can truly elicit the best information from people when you need it;
2. **Recognize that people need connections to thrive** – if a firm's best assets go down in the elevator each night, those assets are only at their best when they are able to make meaningful connections and relationships. Relationships, that can, in time, bear fruit for a firm by way of HUMINT. Give people time to connect outside of work, encourage attendance at networking events with no purpose other than to make connections and allow the firm's network to grow;
3. **Cast a wide net** – when opportunities at the firm present themselves, the instinct is to only involve management in the decision-making, but there are connections throughout the firm at every level. When faced with a decision or a strategic priority that will be informed by HUMINT (and they all should!), be sure to reach out beyond the usual suspects for connection. There may be personal connections to a situation that are not captured in a firm's CRM which can lead to a conversation with a key decision-maker that would have otherwise been left unknown. The same goes for talking to business partners and reviewing social media connections/followers; and
4. **HUMINT is manual but effective**. While we choose to rely on technology as much as possible and with good reason, HUMINT is a manual, person-to-person activity. It requires knowing people, talking to people and eliciting information effectively. It takes time and patience to do it well and to see the best benefits from HUMINT; however, when executed properly, it can mean the difference between a successful venture and a failed one.

It's a relationship business

Successful AI relies on the ability to reduce data – structured and unstructured – to a series of repeatable tasks. AI can drive financial decisions, strategic decisions, marketing campaigns and sales efforts. But AI today fails in its ability to provide insightful commentary. AI cannot read context nor match the qualitative aspects of the market to what individuals say or do. Insights backed by practised and effective HUMINT alongside CI analysis can help law firms with the "act of seeing into a situation," thereby increasing the unique competitive advantage. In a world where technology is the reigning innovator, firms that are able to harness the power of *who they know* will continue to be successful. We know that the legal business is based on relationships. Clients will follow partners, not firms. Long-standing institutional clients will stay with firms they have been with for years on the strength of those relationships alone.

The world in 2019 is changing, and new technologies like AI continue to evolve and effect the practice of law – from billing to realization, from matter mapping to predicting ligation outcomes. There is no doubt that the business of law is not immune to the effects of technology, but the legal business is still built on trust, and trust is built on relationships between people. While intelligence is issue-based, insights are people-based, and (at the least for the moment!) this continues to be an industry run by people.

Chapter 4: Creating an AI-powered alliance between marketing and knowledge services

By David Kamien, CEO of Mind-Alliance Systems

This chapter describes ways to enhance collaboration between a law firm's marketing and knowledge services departments and their business intelligence, research and knowledge management teams. Collaboration between these groups and others, such as the IT department, increases profitability, drives revenue growth, and maximizes the value of the support provided to attorneys and the value that the firm provides to clients. Effective teamwork collaboration will enable BD-related groups to help the firm's attorneys retain clients and attract prospects by becoming trusted experts and advisors for critical issues.

In our view, combining people, process, and technology is the key to a law firm's ability to distill the most critical expertise from a sea of data, and proactively integrate intelligence into BD decision-making. Equipped with AI-powered predictive analytics tools, analysts can more efficiently and proactively deliver the intelligence that attorneys and clients need, when they need it. Advanced collaborative intelligence systems provide a competitive edge because they increase the firm's ability to:

- Spot more opportunities in the business environment, before competitors;
- Develop a more comprehensive understanding of what clients need and determine synergies with a company; and
- Develop stronger value propositions and client relationships.

Building smart collaboration between law firm organizations and their teams is a difficult undertaking. A variety of organizational culture, process, data, and governance issues can undermine the effectiveness of collaboration and the efficiency of knowledge use in the context of law firm marketing and BD intelligence efforts. However, tackling the organizational dynamics and data management challenges involved is worth the effort, as it enables firms to achieve marketing and BD results that would otherwise be out of reach. Heidi Gardner, the author of *Smart Collaboration* (2017), has found that the more disciplines that are involved in a client engagement, the higher the annual average revenue. We now turn to solutions to address the most common and crucial problems.

Leadership and culture

The first place law firms often turn is to technology, but leadership and culture are often the keys to unlocking better collaboration. Although marketing, knowledge services and IT teams may work for the same law firm, they have different subcultures. Each department may be different in terms of values, assumptions, beliefs, practices, workplace habits, interaction patterns, work styles, the degree of participation in meetings and decision-making, and styles of conflict resolution. The cultures of different units might not be fully compatible in terms of the degree of centralization, the degree of conformity, deference to authority, adherence to rules, and symbols of power and status. Some of these factors may undermine collaboration with other groups.

For example, a firm culture that allows marketing people to act as higher-status gatekeepers who guard their relationships with busy partners can frustrate research analysts. In law firms with distributed teams, it is not always practical to invite representatives from every relevant support group to every face-to-face meeting or call with a partner to discuss marketing and BD strategy. However, to be able to provide proactive intelligence support, a good research analyst naturally wants and needs to develop a profound understanding of a partner's context and information needs. When a knowledge services organization interacts with patrons, its business intelligence, research and knowledge management professionals glean experiential information which informs future work, professional development, and the purchasing of new research products. Its broad awareness of the business of the firm enables a KS team to provide proactive intelligence support which helps spot potential BD opportunities. When BD team members provide the knowledge services team with the context around a research request (the "why"), it influences the scope and quality of the product. It also influences how the request is archived, which can enrich and expand the knowledge base of the firm.

Business development professionals are under a lot of pressure because they are now expected to both execute the day-to-day operational needs of an effective marketing and BD strategy, and to proactively source opportunities and identify potential roadblocks to client growth. BD staff are often too busy to source, evaluate and interpret real-time information from scores of available external research sources, so they easily can miss important information.

Collaboration between BD and knowledge management teams fluent in the drivers of business and the competitive landscape, at the individual and practice area levels, makes BD and lead generation strategies more effective.

BD and KS teams both have firm-wide views and are well-positioned to "connect the dots" on opportunities across individual lawyers within the firm, offices and practice areas. However, they are challenged by the lack of a centralized repository of real-time information to support appropriate distribution and analysis.

A group dynamics assessment by an organizational psychologist can provide a snapshot of norms, expectations, levels of engagement, and views on the quality of leadership and clarity of goals. Whenever you ask law firm departments to change their people's behavior, you are dealing with organizational psychology. Interviewing the top of an organization's leadership reveals what is working well and what keeps people up at night. Conducting an audit of group dynamics shows how well groups function in terms of psychology, and communication audits reveal networks and information flows.

People need to understand the profiles, strengths, and weaknesses of the groups and individuals with whom they need to work. Studies conducted by Dr Larry Richard of over 5000 attorneys revealed that the psychological profiles of attorneys are quite uniform across firms, as compared with the average scores for non-lawyers. It can be helpful to train non-lawyer service providers on how to effectively pitch ideas to and meet the needs of lawyers.

Lay the foundation for strategic alignment

The departments that support marketing and BD efforts should harmonize their strategies, processes, and systems. Marketing and knowledge services directors can start by aligning their teams around a shared understanding of the firm's overarching business priorities and each department's strategies and processes for jointly achieving them.

Departments need to understand each other department's capabilities and harness them to achieve the firm's highest-priority business objectives. Department leaders must develop joint strategies to achieve these objectives, make progress towards shared goals, and define performance metrics for the outcomes towards which they are jointly working.

Marketing and research teams have well-aligned processes for any given practice group, attorney, or thematic BD initiative area ("Sell more M&A services to fintech companies in NY"). They can immediately identify the people responsible for producing each intelligence product needed at each phase of the practice group's BD process.

Department leaders should create the policy, management and technical conditions needed to achieve better collaboration between their teams:

- Articulate shared goals and craft plans for achieving them together;
- Communicate a clear and persuasive vision for collaboration and total commitment to partnership;
- Provide the authority and legitimacy for action and build support in the environment;
- Ensure managers lead by example and model the collaboration behavior they want to instill into their teams;
- Send a powerful message to everyone by documenting leaders' shared commitment to collaboration in a joint MoU or mission statement;
- Identity factors that conflict with the goals of collaboration;
- Identify barriers to trust among participants and any perceived inequities in effort versus benefit in system participation;
- Craft policies, performance evaluation, and reward systems that are supportive of collaboration concurrent with joint accomplishments;
- Define strategies to eliminate or minimize discrepancies in effort/ benefit and rewarding people who contribute extra work;
- Motivate, build commitment, guide activities, and encourage creativity and innovation;
- Mobilize resources;
- Build trust among people and groups that are expected to collaborate;
- Establish mechanisms – typically starting with face-to-face meetings – for establishing and reinforcing personal working relationships;
- Put incentives in place to reward communication and collaboration so people believe they will personally gain from collaboration,

save them time, increase their personal impact, and enhance their careers;
- Develop a shared lexicon; and
- Post transparent rules of engagement.

In addition, department leaders should make sure everyone understands relationships and dependencies between teams, team members' backgrounds and capabilities, team business rules, relationships, and dependencies.

Other steps to ensure successful collaboration include deliberately planning and coordinating interactions between support groups in ways that make BD more systematic and shift research services from a reactive to a proactive posture. Furthermore, department leaders need to develop a shared understanding of each practice group's different growth priorities and unique experience, and identify problematic relationships among people that need to collaborate, and identify past successes or failures in interdepartmental collaboration.

Marketing, knowledge services and other support group leaders in most law firms will not undertake the change management initiative required to build effective collaboration between their departments. That is why a law firm's leaders – top administrators, managing partners, practice group chairs, chief information officers, training directors, and chief innovation officers – have a critical governance role to play in strengthening the collaborative BD intelligence capabilities of the firm. They need to provide the personnel, financial resources, technical resources, and training. They need to set policy and establish governance mechanisms to ensure that goals for collaboration are achieved.

Top management should hold practice group leaders accountable for specifying criteria for targeting, spotting, vetting and ranking BD opportunities. Without that accountability, the resources of marketing and research teams will be unfocused and suboptimal, even if they do collaborate well.

Harmonize intelligence processes and product strategies

At the operational level, marketing and research teams (leaders, functional specialists, IT specialists and analysts) need to develop shared models of their business processes: the collections of related, structured activities performed by one or several organizations to produce a specific service, product or business result. They can depict these business processes using graphical tools or by drawing them on a white board and documenting them in prose narrative. The key is to agree on an achievable idealized ("to-be") process and on the steps needed to close the gap with the current (as-is) capabilities in a strategically prioritized way.

Multiple departments and roles create dozens of types of intelligence products and research services that support strategic marketing and operational BD decision-making. The process of ordering, producing, and consuming intelligence products and services should be a central focus of the effort to align interdepartmental alignment and coordination. Without coordination, research deliverables are often provided inconsistently, in a reactive fashion, and without harnessing all available expertise and data. As a result, the support provided is far less timely and valuable to requestors than it might be. A useful first step can be creating a shared catalog of standard intelligence products and research services and mapping each type of product and service to the roles responsible for producing them and the data sources used as inputs. Creating an intelligence product and research service catalog is an opportunity to define product and quality of service levels.

Gathering the necessary information, participating in group discussions, resolving differences, and reaching decisions during business process modeling and alignment effort is labor- and time-intensive. It requires a high level of commitment from all participants and organizations. When creating the process models, the participating teams need to share information about how they work, including activities, roles, tasks, phases, meetings, communication, and schedules. Therefore, it is usually a good idea to pick a practice group or two, focus on the most common and valuable intelligence products. Another practical step is to create a glossary of terms and to develop a controlled vocabulary for roles, activities, BD process phases, IT systems, knowledge products and research services.

It is important to involve customers, as well as knowledge professionals. Mapping and studying the intelligence customer's user journey in requesting and using intelligence products is a powerful exercise. Consider asking intelligence product owners and knowledge service providers questions such as:

1. Are intelligence products and research services offered proactively? Is it easy for busy attorneys and BD staff to order the ones that they need?

2. Do the intelligence products contain the insights that partners and BD people need to impress clients? If the products and services produced are not as valuable as they need to be it may be reflected in attorneys not reading email alerts, newsletters, and company profiles; and
3. How can the products and services be made more valuable and produced more efficiently?

An inexpensive and effective way of improving collaboration between teams is to have representatives from each team produce training manuals and handbooks on topics such as the following:

- How to do BD for practice group X;
- When and how to use subscription data resources for practice group X;
- How to use internal firm data to understand a firm's substantive legal experience;
- How to prepare for a BD strategy meeting;
- How to produce standard BD intelligence products (e.g., industry and company profiles);
- How to submit clear requests for BD and knowledge services support; and
- How easily can BD staff customize standard BD research products?

How to synchronize processes

Annual scenario exercises provide an experiential learning opportunity for all participants in the BD process to learn how marketing, BD and research teams need to collaborate. First, the relevant stakeholders should develop a scenario involving a fictitious target prospect (either an existing client that is a target for cross-selling, or an entirely new prospect). Conduct a simulation to ensure that everyone shares understanding about the involvement of different groups and how their processes intersect.

The group should go through every phase of the BD process from planning and research to marketing communication efforts. All stakeholders should explain how they provide actionable input at each BD phase and to describe how that could improve, enhance, or create the current BD

Research Artifacts and processes. This exercise will foster a better shared understanding of their division of labor and interdependencies.

In **regularly scheduled BD strategy meetings**, everyone involved in delivering intelligence products and services that support BD can synchronize their activities. These BD strategy and coordination meetings should leverage the perspectives, experience, expertise, and imagination of all participants. That way the group can design bespoke intelligence initiatives and proactively suggest innovative ways they can support strategic decision making and BD efforts with CI, BI and data resources.

The knowledge services team can craft **research plans for the specific types of opportunities** that each practice group and partner seeks. They can work to identify the events that indicate potential opportunity (e.g., litigation) before competing law firms spot them. For example, stock price movements and insider trades could indicate potential opportunities for securities fraud litigation work. Research departments and data scientists can set up systems for the monitoring and analysis of these indicators.

AI-powered BD intelligence applications

One of the biggest challenges law firms face in building intelligent BD knowledge systems is accessing high-quality data from disparate systems so it can be efficiently analyzed. Many law firms don't have enough analysts to cope with the growing volume of BD research requests. For most law firms, "throwing more people at the problem" is not a viable solution. Analysts spend hours each week manually searching disparate internal IT systems and external data sources and pasting information into a report or email template. Valuable time and expertise is used to gather information, to organize that information, and transfer it from one system to another or – even worse – to an entirely separate information artifact, such as a spreadsheet or text document. In a system with limited and costly resources, there is significant incentive to recover this time by using more efficient tools that automate much of the gathering and integration of disparate data and information sources, thereby turning information into actionable knowledge.

In addition, the enterprise must consider opportunity costs of missing information. Information may be missed for several reasons. Gathering information from multiple, heterogeneous sources is prone to errors, either by missing information or errors in transferring that information from its original source system or database into another. The interconnections between data and information elements are not always obvious and making those connections correctly is also prone to error, even by skilled personnel working on systems they know well. Finally, there are deeper connections among data elements that can only be reasonably discerned through the use of advanced analytics. Machine learning and AI techniques have demonstrated benefit in uncovering meaningful, business-centric relationships that can deliver impact to a business.

Basic company profiles with a fixed set of data elements can be generated automatically via integration with electronic resources. Business background reports can be templated, ordered on demand by busy attorneys (or better yet, offered proactively), and produced more efficiently if the production processes are standardized. Experienced analysts should work on intelligence deliverables that only they can deliver.

We also argue that the current, highly manual process of sifting through large bodies of data and information trapped in a variety of information systems is unsustainable going forward. The amount of data generated that is relevant to business problems in the legal industry is accelerating. In addition, the breadth of information, the various types of information that can be leveraged for BD benefit, and for the benefit of other parts of the organization, is also growing. As has been said, throwing more resource at this problem is not a sustainable solution, as the information landscape continues to explode. Traditional tools – such as relational databases and document stores – are inefficient for the task of information integration. The emergence of mature knowledge graph tools provides the opportunity to integrate data efficiently and effectively, and in a manner that is focused directly on providing value for specific, identified business problems. Knowledge graphs are also a flexible technology that allows for quick extension of the knowledge base to leverage new information elements as they become available in this rich information age.

Looking a bit further out, knowledge graphs will provide a substrate for "what if" scenarios. As has been discussed, it is important that the traditional questions asked must be answered in a more efficient and accurate manner; however, it is also important to enable information researchers to explore other questions as they may arise in an interactive manner rather than with projects that require significant resource over sustained periods of time.

Just-in-time semantic integration will be a key discriminator in separating successful businesses from those who lag behind as we move into an ever-richer information- and knowledge-centric future.

Data challenges

Numerous data integration, data quality, and data management issues undermine a law firm's ability to leverage advanced analytics, reporting, and data visualization of the data. Here are some examples:

- Internal enterprise systems and external subscription sources are often only accessible via a graphical user interface which people have to search manually rather than an application programming interface (API) that a computer can access;[1]
- Content licensing agreements often undermine the usage scenarios for subscription data;
- Each data resource has its own data schema that typically does not conform to a standard that defines the meaning of each metadata element;
- Integrating data in an ad-hoc, point-to-point way, is time-consuming and expensive. Data lakes can be useful, but enterprise knowledge graphs are better because they map the metadata from the integrated sources to ontologies – formal knowledge representations that support machine reasoning; and
- Many firms lack policies for data collection, use, storage and handling and data quality standards and dictionaries. They have limited documentation about databases and systems of record.

Given that each law firm has different BD processes and combinations of internal and external IT systems and data sources. Software products such as CRM and intranet software platforms aren't designed to support semantic data integration or the creation of "expert systems" based on formal/ontological models, reasoning engines, and rules. They do not structure knowledge in a way that enables the system to support natural language question-answering ("Identify all attorneys who are veterans, speak Spanish, and have experience with pharma M&A transactions over $1bn) or machine reasoning and predictive modeling ("Which companies will become the most profitable clients?").

The potential benefits of predictive modeling and semantic reasoning are significant, and are achievable. However, achieving success in these areas is highly dependent on the availability of large quantities of high-quality data. The implication is that information integration work, in addition to being efficient, must also produce quality data and information products. We will not discuss the technical details in this chapter, but suffice it to say that the details make all the difference. Machine learning (ML) algorithms and semantic analytics produce actionable insights only as effective as the quality of the data over which those algorithms operate.

That is why leading law firms are starting to build BD intelligence software systems powered by knowledge graphs and machine reasoning. Knowledge graphs are knowledge bases that leverage a formal (machine readable) representation of complex relationships between entities (e.g. companies, people). Thanks to their graph structure, KGs have a sheer performance advantage when querying connected data versus relational databases and NoSQL stores (e.g. "data lakes"). Most importantly, knowledge graphs store data in a connected way that facilitates more efficient discovery of semantic and context dependencies between entities than in SQL and NoSQL databases. The more data sources are added and contextualized, the more intelligent a solution becomes.

Knowledge graphs can power solutions that deliver more relevant and enriched answers to natural language questions posed by users that require a high degree of context understanding. Naturally, knowledge graphs need to be based on high-quality, rich, and detailed data and deep domain understanding.

The knowledge graph and the "live" BD intelligence application they support will enable the marketing and knowledge services teams to more systematically integrate intelligence into each phase of the BD process. Applications powered by AI can help users apply best practices in BD and become more proactive by suggesting next BD action steps, along with the associated research services, data resources, and people with relevant experience to invite projects. With a knowledge graph based on reliable data, a law firm can use machine reasoning and predictive models, for example to prioritize target prospect based on expected profitability.

Conclusion

Over the coming years, we expect increasing competition in the market for legal services to drive rapid evolutionary change. Law firm leaders will expect ever-higher levels of BD and RS process efficiency, enabled by effective interdepartmental collaboration and advanced software systems. The next generation of BD managers and research analysts will be digital natives who grew up with real-time collaboration software apps. They will be at the vanguard of transforming legacy processes and systems into a more effective symbiosis of people and machines, one that contributes immensely to the firm's revenue growth and profitability.

The author would like to acknowledge the valuable inputs provided by Luke Ferrandino and Gina Lynch, CMO and director of knowledge services at Paul, Weiss, Rifkind, Wharton & Garrison LLP; Scott Bailey, research services director at Eversheds Sutherland; and Todd Corham, chief information officer at Saul Ewing Arnstein & Lehr.

Reference

1. We recommend that research services directors learn to negotiate smart deals with data providers to get API as well as GUI access and data processing rights.

Chapter 5: The use of artificial intelligence by leading firms in client-facing work – a survey

By Yolanda Cartusciello, partner at PP&C Consulting

In late 2017, my consulting firm, PP&C Consulting, was hired by a client to assess whether and how elite law firms were employing artificial intelligence in client-facing work. The client trusted me to define "elite law firms" and did not dictate a set of firms to be interviewed. As part of the assessment, the client wanted to better understand the way in which firms were thinking about the development of artificial intelligence over the next five to ten years and what place it might take in the legal industry. The client also asked us to explore the extent to which firms were using artificial intelligence or big data in their pricing and project management efforts.

Over the past few months, I've had the opportunity to update my findings through conversations with about half of the original participants as well as a few additional "elite law firms". The following is a summary of the general results of the original assignment, updated to reflect the new findings.

Survey subjects

In 2017, I interviewed CIOs, directors of IT, directors of KM, and "innovation partners" at 22 law firms, as well as a founder of a subsidiary consulting firm of one law firm. At several firms we spoke with two representatives, as the firms had divided responsibilities between innovation partners, IT and KM.

I supplemented these findings with 15 conversations in February of 2019, 12 of which were with original participants and three of which were with new participants. These updated findings reflect conversations with 25 firms in total. All participating firms were Am Law 50 or Global 100 firms and further broke down as:

- Eight national firms;
- Five global firms;
- Six New York firms;
- Three Magic Circle firms; and
- Three California firms.

As part of both sets of discussions, I promised anonymity, which allowed participants to speak more openly.

Summary findings

There has been much hype about the advent of the use of artificial intelligence (AI) in the practice of law. The reality is that even the most innovative firms are in the early stages of developing AI. The elite firms we surveyed are, for the most part, engaging in efforts to understand the technology, creating pilots of various software and developing a philosophy about how and when such technology should be incorporated and deployed within their organizations.

Although the most advanced of the firms surveyed have solidified their philosophies, the difference between their use and deployment of the technology versus other firms surveyed is not as significant as one might be led to believe by the marketing efforts of those firms. Complicating the landscape further is the fact that many technology vendors and law firms are defining the term "artificial intelligence" broadly enough to include technology that has been available and in use for many years.

Currently, law firm use of AI is mainly limited to tasks where it would be beneficial to review large volumes of information for similar or anomalous attributes. Some areas of practice have lent themselves more readily to this automation (e-discovery, for example) and therefore adoption by firms is higher and occurred further back than has been the case for other areas (e.g. due diligence or contract review in the M&A context).

While the use cases and success stories across firms tend to center around efficiencies gained by the use of AI, the firm strategy and the marketing of AI capabilities are markedly different amongst those firms that view themselves as on the AI cutting-edge from those that see AI as primarily an efficiency tool. Ironically, although the former group may indeed be ahead, it is likely the firm attitude and commitment that will help them advance more quickly and gain real marketing advantage from their efforts.

When I originally spoke with participants in 2017, I concluded that any firm surveyed could, with some effort and investment, overtake any other firm in the development and deployment of AI in legal work, primarily because the function is so nascent, and no one firm had moved that far ahead. I continue to believe that we are still in the early stages of use of AI in legal work; however, I think the leading firms are already showing progress in pulling away from the rest of the pack, and it will be harder now for firms in the lagging group to catch up without significant investment of time and resources.

In the short time between the original survey and this update, several of the original participants have made significant additional investments and have engaged in new ventures and experiments in the use of AI in client-facing work.

The implications of those investments, coupled with pressure from clients to reduce costs and gain efficiencies, signals the advent of a shift in how legal services and advice will be delivered, including how the leverage model and the recruitment of training of young talent will evolve over the next five years.

Law firms would do well to pay particular attention to how AI can be part of the solution and help them bond even more closely with current clients as well as attract new clients.

The similarities among firms

Given the vast differences in the sizes of firms, practice emphases, governing approaches, and administrative structures of the firms interviewed, one might have expected more pronounced differences in the adoption of artificial intelligence as a client-facing tool. While there are enough differences to categorize firms into three groupings (described later in this report), on balance, it appears that the similarities tend to outweigh the differences.

These similarities stem from two important factors:

1. As the technology itself is still nascent and generic, even the most aggressive firms are not yet able to capitalize on a distinct differentiated artificial intelligence capability;[1] and
2. It takes a significant commitment of time and energy of practicing lawyers to help outside vendors and technologists customize the technology to make it useful within the law firm environment.

We summarize some of the basic similarities below:

Budget

The similarities begin with the dollars devoted to the research and development of artificial intelligence tools and software, with most firms reporting that they are devoting less than five percent of their tech budget to this area. No firm surveyed had trouble justifying spend in this area, and none attributed slow adoption to lack of budget.

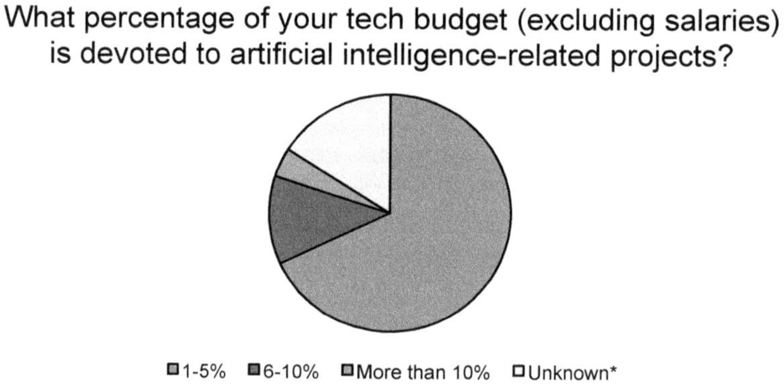

*Figure 1: AI allocation of law firm tech budgets. *Some firms have a separate budget for innovation-related projects that expands across the firm.*

Respondents caution, however, that the tools themselves are relatively inexpensive at this juncture and that the lawyer manpower needed to train and customize the tools is where the hidden costs reside. Some respondents further indicated that they couldn't quantify the cost by percentage of their own budget because this initiative was sitting on another budget (often referred to as a firmwide "innovation" budget). They expected the hard costs to continue to be attributed to a different budget for at least the next few years.

Engagement levels

Even if some firms are still in the pilot stage, every firm but one indicated that they have undertaken some initiative in the use of artificial intelligence for client-facing work.

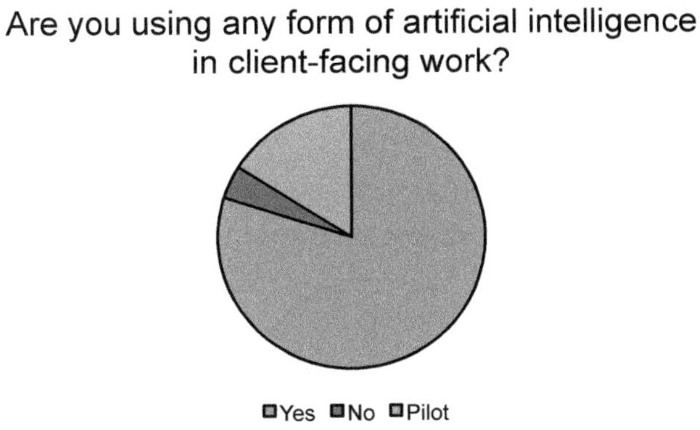

Figure 2: AI usage in client-facing work

Not surprisingly, there is more penetration in the litigation (discovery) realm, where software development and usage is the most mature.

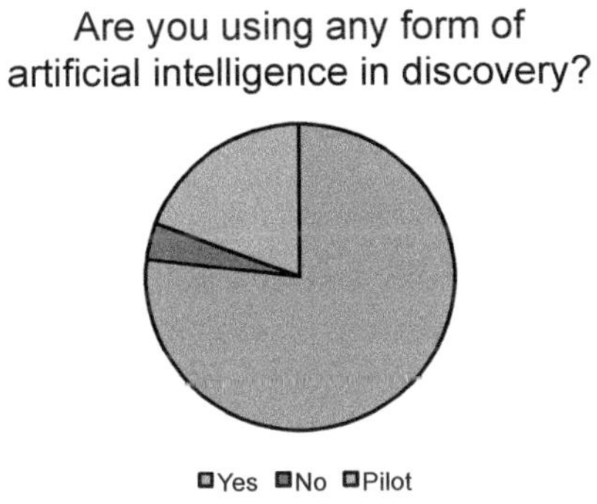

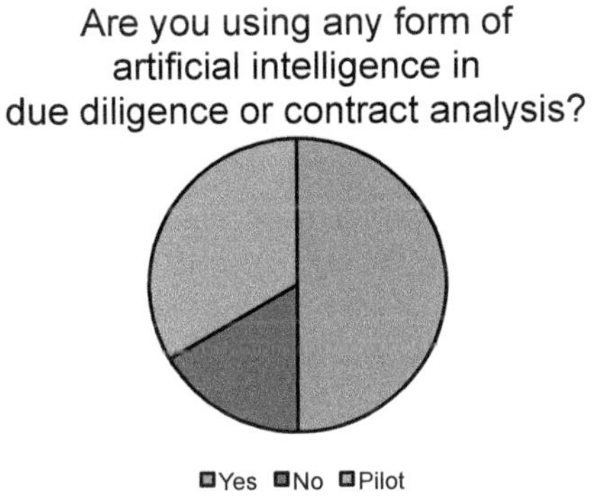

Figure 3: Practice area use of AI

Even the firms that appear to be on the cutting edge concede that no firm has figured out the best way to use this technology to support client-facing work. This partly due to the immaturity of the technology applications for the legal sector, and partly because firms and clients lack experience in managing and parsing projects in a way that would make meaningful use of the technology.

However, those firms that are coupling their pilot AI programs with other forms of service models (e.g. joining forces with other organizations or employing former in-house counsel to work on such projects) appear to be gaining some traction.

Additionally, few firms are reporting use of artificial intelligence or big data analysis for pricing or project management work. For most firms, these are newer functions; some of the firms surveyed don't have project management functions at all.

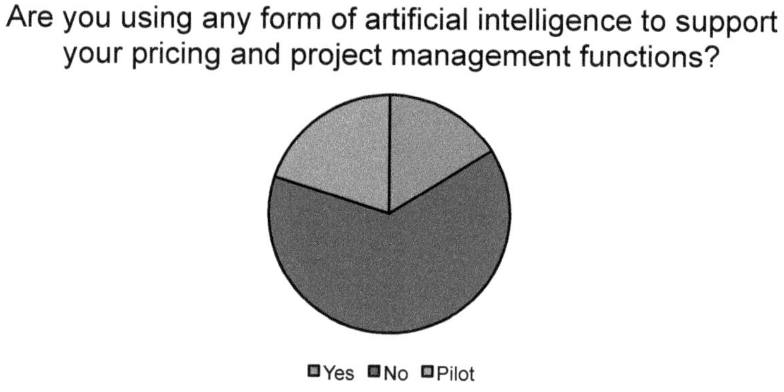

Figure 4: Pricing and project management AI

When pressed to describe further, those firms that answered "yes" indicated that it was not much more than using tools like Redwood to help them better mine the data for trends. One firm did indicate that they had made real progress in using big data to help in pricing work, in particular, using AI tools to better parse out the cost of specific phases of matters. Still, the big obstacle to using big data in pricing and project management work is not the software or technology, but rather the state of the data. In most firms, the data is not parsed or cleansed enough to make any analysis meaningful. Many of the firms I spoke with a second time indicated they've spent significant time and resources to start cleaning up their financial data and to put parameters on how the information is collected and coded for better data mining.

Build or buy

There is universal consensus that firms will and should work with third-party vendors who bring a level of technological expertise in this area that most firms cannot begin to match. Respondents believe that it's part of their job to help the vendors become more sophisticated about the legal sector, which will, in turn, give an advantage to those firms that helped shape the technology. Interestingly, firms believe that this will still be the model five years from now. Although a few firms are dabbling with some small internal development projects, they've indicated that those tend to be either one-offs or add-ons to the third-party technology.

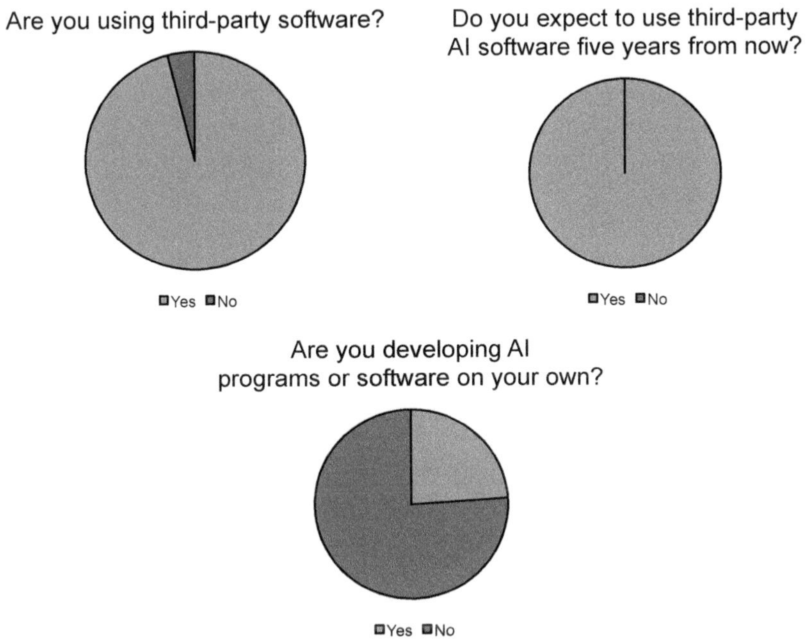

Figure 5: Employment of third-party AI software

Staffing

Firms are making investments of time and money in the area, with most firms adding headcount and borrowing people from other areas to focus on AI.

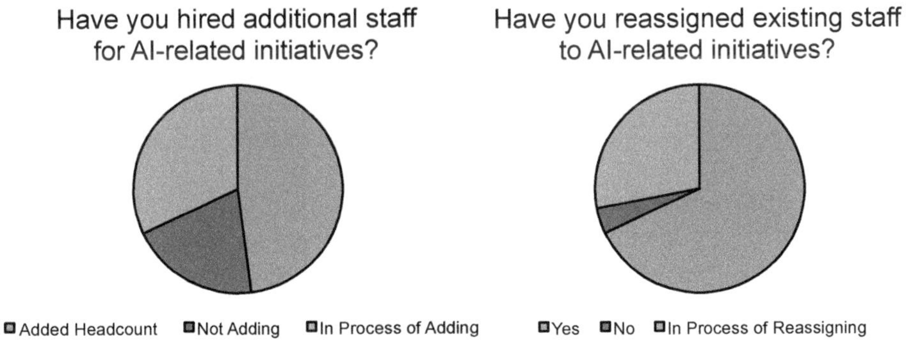

Figure 6: Dedicated AI staffing

New hires in this area include JDs, engineers, coders, project management professionals, and technology professionals with AI deployment experience.

AI teams or AI initiative teams have emerged in most of the IT groups in the firms surveyed. Every firm believes that the AI tech team will grow over the next three to four years. A few firms indicated that it might actually recede at that point, given the firm should be far enough along that they won't need to devote as many resources to a special team as they do now.

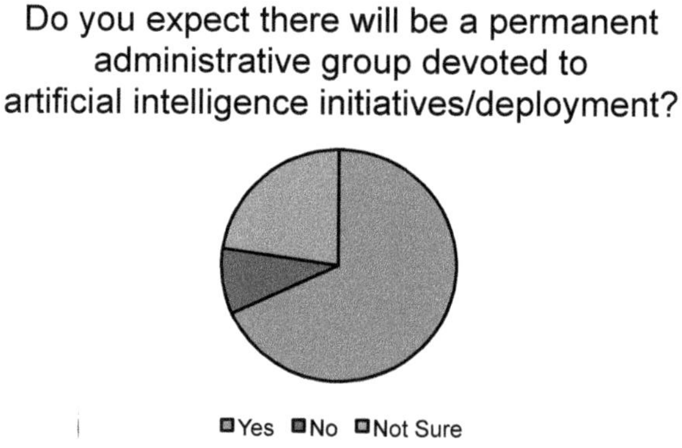

Figure 7: AI permanence

Prioritization of efforts

Much to the consternation of some of the respondents, prioritization of AI-related efforts tend to be based upon the desire of lawyers within certain practices to engage with the technology and tools, rather than upon agreed-upon firm priorities. Most firms have indicated discovery and due diligence as the two highest priority areas at this time.

Some respondents indicated that they are overwhelmed by requests from lawyers to look at certain technologies or tools, while others are initiating the discussions with lawyers about promising tools they've seen.

The differences between firms

Contrasting the similarities between firms, there are some meaningful differences in philosophy and execution of AI-related efforts. Firms fall roughly into three categories. Firms within each of these categories do not line up neatly by size or historic type of firm. You will find traditional Wall Street firms, as well as national and Magic Circle firms, in each of the three categories.

Group one: artificial intelligence as disruption (eight of 25 firms)

"Disruptor" firms within this category see artificial intelligence as a major disruptor in the way in which legal services will be delivered. They believe the disruption is already occurring, but will be most significant in the next three to five years. These firms want to be part of the disruption. The firms with "innovation budgets" separate from other administrative budgets tend to be included in this category, although two firms that indicated they are spending less than five percent of their tech budget on AI are also in this category.

Disruptors indicate that they are striving to get ahead of the curve, making significant investments in this area, both in terms of technology purchase and development as well as time investment, including tech team, KM teams, paralegals and lawyers. They appear to be to be further up the adoption curve, having invested either longer or more intensely. Disruptors also report the greatest number of simultaneous engagements with external vendors to develop or roll out products.

The disruptors espouse the philosophy that they are going to find every way imaginable to engage with this technology. They are pushing for firm-wide adoption and use of AI tools, although they concede they will have some personnel who will have a particular expertise and affinity for working with the technology. Those personnel will be tasked with helping fee-earners interact with the technology as opposed to interacting with it themselves. One respondent indicated that the firm goal is that within five years, no piece of legal work (including drafting documents, developing strategies) gets touched by a lawyer until it has been touched by some form of AI. During the update discussions, two other firms espoused a very similar sentiment. Every disruptor indicated that they already have "success stories" attributable to the use of AI.

Impact of technology on associate classes

Disruptors are thinking seriously about the impact on their more junior classes. They believe that AI advancement will necessitate a dramatic shift in how junior classes are trained and what kinds of work will give them the experience that they may have otherwise received from assignments that will now be handled by AI tools.

They concede that the size of incoming classes may be rethought as well, since the technology will help to eliminate some of the hourly work that more junior associates would have handled. One participant even said that while it wasn't a deliberate roadmap decision, they've already seen an impact on class size. Another indicated that they are "getting close" to adjusting incoming class size as a result of AI-related efficiencies. Yet still another indicated that the size of the classes might not change, but the opportunities for different career paths emanating from the intersection of AI technology and the law may arise.

Pricing

Not surprisingly, given their belief that class size and therefore leverage ratios may be disrupted, disruptors are experimenting with pricing, more so than the firms that fall into other areas. Some disruptors are using fixed-fee models for some of the work, or experimenting with sharing costs of the technology as part of the pricing. Others in this category say that investments of these types are the cost of doing business and that AI investment simply provides protection against pricing erosion.

Perceived opportunities

One disruptor indicated that AI-related investments may lead to different kinds of work for law firms (e.g. project management for clients).

Several disruptors have developed or are considering developing consulting subsidiaries or arms that will eventually support the use of this technology. One of these firms expects to offer its consulting services to other law firms, not just in-house teams. Another disruptor indicated that they have already been hired by an in-house department to help them reengineer the in-house department processes as a result of a combination of their AI pilot programs and an exclusive arrangement they've made with a consulting firm.

Disruptors are already marketing their AI capabilities to their clients. Innovation partners say they are proactively visiting clients to talk about what the firm is able to do with AI-related technology and how that impacts the bottom line as well as the timeline and outcomes of matters.

Client pressure

Every disruptor indicated they were getting "intense" pressure from clients to do more in this area, beyond just RFP questions.

A word about "superdisruptors"

It is worth noting that even within the disruptor group, there are three firms that are distinctively advanced in their efforts. These firms are either (1) collaborating with universities to advance the relationship between AI and the legal profession; (2) collaborating with clients on AI-related projects; and/or (3) collaborating with other kinds of professional service organizations to create joint "AI and service" related offerings.

Group two: artificial intelligence as efficiency (12 of 25 firms)

"Efficiency" firms see artificial intelligence as a support tool in the same way that LexisNexis and Westlaw are support tools. They do not expect AI to supplant lawyers in a meaningful way, but –similar to LexisNexis' effect on the practice of law – expect AI to make lawyers more efficient and accurate in their work. They believe "human+machine" will be better than human. Efficiency firms are already working extensively with AI-related tech in the litigation space (primarily discovery) and are now trying to work with it in the corporate area (primarily M&A due diligence). Even within this group, firms are reporting "success stories" – in particular, using litigation discovery tools.

Efficiency firms tend to keep the technology a little more closely held within a team composed of tech, KM and a small group of lawyers. Many of these firms believe that this group will become (or already has become) a permanent team within the firm. Some have indicated that this group will become a separate function within the firm and will be marketed to clients as such. These firms believe that aspects of the technology might be distributed more widely within the lawyer population, but for the most part the average lawyer will not be expected to master the technology. In the early years, however, many lawyers from across the firm will be expected to "teach" the technology how to better help the lawyers.

Impact of technology on associate classes

Efficiency firms have spent some time thinking about the impact on lawyers, especially the junior classes, but have come to no conclusions yet on how this will impact the training or size of the class. Several concede that the impact on class size is inevitable.

Pricing

These firms are also strongly considering pricing ramifications and some have played with the pricing. However, most believe their firm brand is strong enough to make a persuasive argument that while other firms may have the same technology and employ it in the same way, these firms have superior lawyers who will be teaching and interacting with the technology, which means that the results will be better. They liken it to the use of LexisNexis or Westlaw. Those same databases are available to everyone. What makes these firms better is not the strength of the database, but of the people analyzing the data and making the judgments on behalf of their clients.

Opportunities

Efficiency firms originally interviewed indicated that they might be slightly behind the disruptors, but believe they have the opportunity to capitalize on the work disruptors have already engaged in to help improve the technology currently available. During the most recent conversations, they indicated that they've almost caught up.

Some efficiency firms believe the development of a combination tech/lawyer group which focuses on AI is a feature that they may be able to market to their clients. They believe some clients will want to work directly with that group to help clients adopt AI technology.

Some efficiency firms believe that AI adoption and use in their firm will be an important marketing component as they strive to differentiate themselves from other elite firms.

Client pressure

Firms in this category are reporting some client interest or mild pressure from clients.

Group three: artificial intelligence as something we need to do (five of 25 firms)

"Something" firms are in the early stages of building their philosophies and engaging in pilot programs. They know they need to do "something" but are unsure what impact AI will have on the legal industry. They agree that efficiency is likely to be one of the major impacts. They think there may be more but are too early in their efforts to espouse specific beliefs. Most of these firms have committees that are focusing time and energy on figuring out what AI will mean to their firm. They are deliberating carefully and moving more slowly.

Some of these firms are reporting cultural aversion by the lawyers. Therefore, they are engaging in side-by-side comparisons of completing the work in the current fashion and using the technology to demonstrate the capabilities of the technology. None blamed the slow adoption on budgetary approval issues. None are reporting client pressure. These firms have not yet started considering the impact on lawyer class sizes or training, nor are they thinking about a pricing model.

Reference

1. However, the use of AI as part of an overall firm strategy to explore alternative models of service are producing interesting and promising signs of progress.

Chapter 6:
Birth of the competitive intelligence department – selling, planning, and managing

By Mark Gediman, reference librarian at Alston & Bird LLP

I grasped the knob of the conference room door, my palm damp with nervous sweat. I had done my research, talked to colleagues and crafted my pitch, backed by 23 PowerPoint slides. Now was the moment of truth: my chance to convince the executive committee to support the establishment of a competitive intelligence service within the library, staffed with a competitive intelligence librarian. An hour later, I had the approval I needed to move forward. The real work then began...

A lot of planning went into that meeting. Questions needed to be anticipated, plans made, and workflows charted. The presentation was painstakingly put together to illustrate the elements of the proposal to complement the oral presentation. Discussing the defined terms, detailed workflow, and the value of this service made a positive impression on the committee.

An important piece of the proposal was developing a common definition of competitive intelligence and demonstrating its value to business development. This was key to managing expectations. Here are some of the points I made in the proposal:

Acquiring clients is a challenge for most attorneys. Generally speaking, law schools do not train attorneys to be salespeople; they are trained to spot issues and solve problems. The unique perspective of their audience is what makes law firm competitive intelligence professionals different from their corporate counterparts. Their task is to identify issues experienced by potential clients.

Law firm management has most likely heard about competitive and business intelligence, and there may even be competitive intelligence performed on an *ad hoc* basis. However, the following questions need to be asked to determine if the current process (if one exists) is providing what the firm needs:

1. Does the firm know what their competitors are doing?
2. Who performs (or will perform) competitive intelligence research?
3. Is the firm routinely examining their clients' needs to see how they align with the firm's practices?
4. Does a process exist for requesting intelligence briefings?
5. Are business developments outcomes tracked and analyzed to ensure that the right information is being provided?

Let's start with this great definition from the Strategic and Competitive Intelligence Professionals association (SCIP, formerly known as the Society of Competitive Intelligence Professionals), circa 2008, which still holds true today:

> *Competitive intelligence is a systematic and ethical program for gathering, analyzing, and managing information about the external business environment that can affect a company's plans, decisions, and operations.*

I also like this definition from a chap whose opinion I trust (and happens to have the same name and address as the author):

> *Information ethically gathered and analyzed with the purpose of making the firm more competitive and profitable in an ever-changing marketplace.*

Please note the inclusion of some form of the term "ethical" in both of the above definitions. This is extremely important for both the firm and analyst to understand at the start. Information is gathered only from reputable sources. This does not preclude the use of human intelligence (or HumInt) gathering. Although this is discussed in more detail in the second chapter of this publication, it cannot be stated too often the surreptitious recording of phone calls, dumpster-diving or misrepresenting one's identity are not valid (or ethical!) information collection techniques. Although the other two activities are more straightforward, it is important to note that misrepresentation can be as simple as not identifying who your employer is when asked. Responding with a simple "I'm sorry, I can't disclose that" or terminating the conversation are both acceptable alternatives.

Competitive intelligence and business intelligence are often used interchangeably, but shouldn't be. Gartner Group has a great definition of business intelligence:

> *Business intelligence (BI) is an umbrella term that includes the applications, infrastructure and tools, and best practices that enable access to and analysis of information to improve and optimize decisions and performance.*

As defined above, business intelligence uses internal information and metrics to determine how competitive intelligence is conducted to further the strategic goals of the firm, practice groups and attorneys.

When pitching the value of performing competitive intelligence within the firm, it is helpful to discuss the cultural, internal strategic goals and firm knowledge of the analyst(s). The task of any researcher is to create reports that are relevant to the requesting attorney. Understanding the firm's culture helps when designing the workflow and the reports. Consideration of the strategic goals, as well as knowledge of the unique practice and personal characteristics of the requestor, enables the analyst to include only required information and analysis.

Locating the function

What should this service look like? Who does what and what is their reporting relationship? These are important questions to which I gave serious consideration. The position required a skilled researcher who was not afraid of analyzing the data and was a skilled communicator. These skills are found in journalists, financial analysts, and librarians.

Some of the most skilled competitive intelligence analysts are journalists by training and experience. Their research skills tend to be thorough and intuitive. Their knack for finding important nuggets of information gives the reports a unique value. It is hard to find journalists with the rare combination of law firm experience and are familiar with the unique needs of the audience.

Financial analysts with law firm experience have a unique perspective on law firm operations. They are able to look at competitors' data and easily spot important trends. This group also knows how to communicate this information in way that's tailored to their audience.

First, full disclosure: I am a librarian. Librarians are generally a good fit for these types of positions. They are proficient researchers, they conduct analysis in the course of their research, and they know their audience. As the recipients of regular research requests from attorneys, they have a high-level view of the firm's strategic goals and the unique strengths of each attorney. This allows the researcher to view and analyze the data within this high-level frame of reference. Reports crafted with this in mind are relevant.

Now comes the question of where to place it within the firm's hierarchy. Is this a group within a larger department or an independent stand-alone operation? Three likely homes for this group are marketing/business development, finance, or library/research services/knowledge services. Here are some factors to consider:

1. Which group has deep knowledge of the firm's strategic plan?
2. Which group has experience managing this type of workflow (more on that below)?
3. Which group has access to research resources?

I have seen the competitive intelligence service work very well in the library and business development departments. Analysts with library backgrounds have functioned at a high level in both departments. However, I would give the edge to the library when it comes to managing this type of analyst. They have a similar workflow, similar staff, and have the vast majority of the firm's research resources. This is the route I ended up taking for the reasons I laid out above. Additionally, since I was the library director, this was a forgone conclusion.

That said, the edge mentioned above between library and the business development department is a slight one. Competitive intelligence analysts with library backgrounds have been placed successfully within the business development departments of several NLJ 250 firms. This department is also comfortable for analysts with a journalistic background. Different firm cultures and processes play a large role in the placement of this function. The choice on where it is placed comes down to what works best in your firm.

Managing expectations

As I crafted my presentation, I spent quite a bit of time, effort and thought to setting up the service. I realized that workflow and managing expectations are key components to the success of a competitive intelligence operation. Frustration by the attorneys with delivery times and formats could cause the new service to fail. It's important for the consumers of the information to clearly understand the direct relationship between turnaround time, purpose and the format of the deliverable reports.

Turnaround time is a major factor in managing expectations. The depth, type and quality of the report is directly affected by when it's needed. As a result of looking at this closely, I came up with the following table:

Turnaround time	Deliverable	Contents
Short term (about one hour)	Data dump: very little or no analysis	• Prepackaged reports along the lines of the West Litigation Monitor Suite, Lex Machina, Hoovers or Bloomberg Analytics • Recent news
Same day	Email or short memo: minimal analysis with broad conclusions	• Prepackaged reports along the lines of the West Litigation Monitor Suite, Lex Machina, Hoovers or Bloomberg Analytics • Relevant news
Long term (three to seven days)	Briefing pack: key analysis and findings	• Detailed, in-depth report • Graphs and charts where appropriate • Legal work analysis, both inside the firm and by other firms • Important news relevant to the practice mix of the firm and the strengths of the attorney pitching the work

I used this table to evaluate requests and determine what is possible in the allotted timeframe.

The reason for the report determines which content is included. It is the stated purpose of the report that prevents the use of the same specific template for all requests. Simply put, different purposes call for different reports.

Below is a brief table that shows the different information required:

Purpose	Report format	Types of information
Lunch meeting	Single page	• Company news • Current revenue • Which firms do they use?
Formal pitch meeting	Detailed information and analysis	• Company profile • Which firms do they use? • SWOT analysis
RFP response	Detailed information and analysis	• Profiles of interviewers and executives • Financial analysis • Company's legal challenges • Scope of RFP and how the firm aligns with it • Relevant company news
Lateral evaluation*	Detailed information and analysis	• Practice mix • Representative cases (if applicable) • Presentations • Articles (both written by and about)
Internal RFPs*	Detailed information and analysis	• Clients • Cases filed against • Principals background check

**Supporting documents should be included in these reports for on demand easy access.*

Obviously, this is not an exhaustive list. This table shows that different purposes require custom reports. Templates are useful for reports, but locking in specific types of data can be a challenge.

Looking at these two tables together shows the importance of conducting a thorough intake interview (also known as the reference interview by librarians). This information should also be captured by the intake form. The turnaround time and the purpose are just as important as the research subject. Note that these tables do not stand alone. It's necessary to know what the categories are from both tables in the original request.

Making tables such as these available to the requestors can simplify the intake process. It is very helpful to provide them with information so they know what to expect. Making them aware of how the report is affected by these requirements eliminates surprises from the end result.

I have mentioned workflow a few times in this chapter. Planning out the competitive intelligence service required that I consider how the intake and deliverable process would work. I found that the information on these two charts were integral part of processing and delivering these reports. It was very helpful to actually build a flow chart documenting what would go into the various types of reports. It helped for me to visualize the process to ensure that each report contained useful information, delivered in an easy-to-read format.

Sources of data

External data such as those referenced in the first table (but not limited to these sources) are usually included in these reports. But that's only part of the story. Internal firm data adds an important dimension to the deliverable. The data on internal contacts with the prospective client from contact management systems are commonly included, but another item can be a good source of this data: the document management system, which contains letters, emails, documents and other correspondence that includes the names of companies and contacts. Firm financial systems can identify opportunities for selling new services (aka cross-selling) to existing clients and analytics that can recommend the best team to meet the needs of the RFP.

Collaboration

A word now on collaboration: The word is "imperative." Collaborating across departments can give the new service information on firm operations and strategy, as well as access to subscription services with useful information. Collaboration is imperative to the success of competitive intelligence, regardless of what department it operates from. My first step was to take the marketing director to lunch and ask a simple question: "How can I help you succeed?" I then showed her a mock-up of a briefing pack and asked if this would be something we could provide to the attorneys when responding to RFPs. She decided to give it a try. Thereafter, we met monthly to discuss how useful the reports were, what changes we could make to both the process and the deliverables, and shared the feedback we had received from the attorneys. I also sat down with the chief financial officer. I agreed to add SIC codes to the billing system and I was given access to relevant data they had relating directly to the requested reports. I worked with both departments to develop metrics to track the success of the service. Without working together, the reports would have lacked some important information and would not have evolved into a valuable tailored product.

Conclusion

The workflow I put together turned out to be successful. Communicating the workflow process to the attorneys gave them confidence in the work product. Working with the other departments gave the reports a useful perspective and using metrics gave the firm confidence in the value of the service. My palms still get a bit damp before giving a presentation on the competitive intelligence services, but I'm secure in my knowledge of its value.

Chapter 7:
Informing your AI – the best taxonomy for CI and BD

By Jeff Cohan, knowledge management consultant

Artificial intelligence refers to computing systems which possess advanced pattern recognition and inferential reasoning abilities. In most instances, the generalist will say that these programs perform "machine learning." This is distinguished from traditional computing based on arithmetic logic. As one might imagine, the potential for applying this technology to all sorts of data crawls is tremendous. The AI tool can be deployed using several methods involving various input methods to "teach" it recognition. In the context of CI and BI analysis, this author finds that it is best to employ traditional taxonomy tools to classify documents, and to then use them as a template for further education. The issue to be resolved is how to develop this taxonomy.

Artificial intelligence can work completely by itself to determine and define relationships relevant to a query, or it can be informed by an information professional. The latter speeds up the process and enables it to deliver more relevant results that are focused to a particular concern. AI reasoning is either deductive or inductive. Inductive reasoning is the AI ability to infer relationships; deductive reason is based on rules of logic. Similarly, as learning is generated, there are various levels of supervision and rewarding the correct behaviors.

The trick is to balance the effort spent on the work product to maximize the result. Effort should be aimed at primary logical relationship rules, and the AI can infer the more nuanced. Some time should also be spent testing and reviewing the intelligence for scope and accuracy.

When teaching an artificial intelligence tool, you should consider using a taxonomy that reflects concept classification relevant to business analysis and competitive intelligence gathering activities in a commercial law firm. That taxonomy should reflect the larger process of legal business analytics.

Of course, that's the sizzle on the steak, if you will. The process of business analytics drives value and is the potentially disruptive force that grows and maintain volume of revenue, as well as market share.

Loosely speaking then, one can generally describe these analytic sets. The particulars are organic to your organization, and those particulars drive the ship. However, a general discussion provides a firm enough structure from which to build.

Relationships

Currently in place and very common, most law firm conception of client development and retention include tools which gather and make accessible client relationship information in one place. The tools are often referred to as CRM systems (client relationship management). These are relatively simple tools that are field-segmented and contain fields like company name, contact name, position, etc. Because there is so much data, they often sit on the cloud rather than internal servers. The taxonomy behind which CRM tools are organized can inform the training of an AI system that is pointed toward firm expense accounts, time sheets, email, work product, and other unformatted data. The latter sources generally are not aggregate to the CRM system, so much insight is lost by not including them. AI makes it possible to broaden this knowledge stream.

However, it should be noted that data repositories are only as good as the data entered into the various source. If your firm keeps track of expense accounts for example, it is importasnt that the request forms be data rich and include the affiliations of individuals, whether formal or informal, i.e. Mr X is the significant other of the CEO at ABC company. Mr X is known to us through work where he was adverse to us at former company DEF.

Experience

One doesn't want to reinvent the wheel or duplicate sources that can be easily searched, but not all law firm experience is easily accessed through public sources or commercial databases. It is therefore necessary to look internally for insights into organizational experience and history. For instance, in the public database, one can see that a firm prosecuted a patent for a particular technology, but the public records don't show the names of the individual attorneys who did the work unless one goes in to a prosecution file and looks for the name of the prosecuting attorney. A more elegant solution is to look for the patent number record in the prosecuting clerk's office within the law firm. When AI is pointed toward an internal clerk's docket, one needs to instruct it with a taxonomy that reflects the importance of associating work with workers. In fact, the same issue is present for all sorts of transactional and litigation work where one only sees the final product on the research databases.

In a similar fashion, one sees that some issues are hidden from the final product. They don't appear in the public record. In the context of a deal document, the final product might reflect an agreement, but the work product might involve considerations relevant to environmental torts, product liability, intellectual property, employment law, etc. One would therefore train the AI tool to recognize a taxonomy of deal acquisition – environmental concern-mercury in ground surface water at plant to be acquired. Once AI conceives of these relationships, it can find these and provide greater insight as well.

When one speaks to a quick experiential tool, think in terms of finding quick and readily analogous experiences. It may not be enough to say we have worked with a particular chemical in a products context. It might be better to say that we have considered specific experts and rejected them based on their position, or that we considered different litigations strategies, and settled on...

Triggers

"Trigger" was the horse that Roy Rogers rode in the Westerns. Reportedly, Trigger learned 150 trick cues and could walk 50 feet (15 meters) on his hind legs. Trigger was so strong, smart, quick and intelligent that his ability apparently went to his head. He would bow and promenade at the slightest cause. The people of the day found it cute that he was a ham.

In our world, artificial intelligence is much the same. We can teach it a lot and it can then execute and perceive at a high level. It may not have an ego; owever, good work should be acknowledged and reinforced so that the AI system will continue to recognize triggering events. Just don't give it oats or other treats.

And what are triggering events? Said triggers denote circumstances that will likely create a need for legal services. This is more inferential and requires a higher degree of reasoning to appreciate. So, concretely, when your client is sued or arrested, it is fairly evident that they need representation. There are also many docket alerting services that will tell you this. It's not very advanced. Qualifying the data is. Just because your client was sued, the docket might be joined to others, or be a part of a pre-existing dispute that another firm already has firmly in grasp, etc.

When your contact moves from the position of associate general counsel at client A and becomes the new general counsel at potential client B, that impacts you and calls for a renewed SWOT analysis of the situation (Strengths, Weaknesses, Opportunities, Threats). That's also pretty straightforward. However, what happens when it rains? Floods? Fires? Tax Cuts? Investments? Interest rates change? New laws, case law, or regulations? War? Famine? A predicted occurrence?

Bright minds scan news sources daily. They have the background and sensitivity to ascertain the developments that are of potential value to generate or retain business in the practices they represent, and they then proactively provide analysis. If an AI system is trained properly, it too can find these triggering events, provide context as to why and to whom they are relevant, and then suggest the proper analysis for vetting the development. The advantage of an AI component in this process is that you can feed more data and increase scope and performance to enhance the work product of an analyst group.

The trick is to develop a taxonomy that lets the system know why particular events can trigger actionable intelligence. In military intelligence, that seems straightforward: enemy puts weapons systems in range of your borders, which threatens your security. In CI/BI, however, it can be a bit more nuanced – for example, tax cuts (potential outcome) return money to large corporations, who use said money to acquire smaller innovators to re-stock their product pipeline. You have certain large clients who might find these types of acquisitions attractive. This intelligence is actionable because you might consider positioning yourself to assist them, or marketing this ability to them so that you are top of mind in their considerations. Often, this might involve cross-selling a client, etc. A sophisticated AI system uses the taxonomy you created to relate these concepts together.

Analysis

SWOT is a good one. The traditional tools of lawyers, IRAC and CIRIP, are also good. They are good because we often report to lawyers, and the analysis is familiar to them. The Harvard Business Review and the MIT Sloan Management Review also have a bunch of good analysis models. The great strength of the traditional business school analytic model is that it provides case studies and demonstrates conclusions that might be applied in similar scenarios. This seems exactly like what AI was designed to do.

The point is to train the system to do the analysis to the best of its abilities and for it to provide an explanation of the process it used.

Lawyers' analytic tools appeal to those who have worked in the field and are used to reading brief points. In terms of presentation, it is best to start with a conclusion, and to then state the issue to be resolved and its context as tersely as possible. Rules and assumptions upon which logic are based then must also be stated clearly. An interweaving of these rules and policy should then precede a restated conclusion.

Teaching the AI system to reason and report in this fashion is then the optimal result. At the same time, an AI tool can support all types of analysis that can be gleaned through a proper education in business administration. As the AI administrator, one needs to recognize these tools as demonstrative and use them to train with.

Conclusion

AI won't replace you; it will enhance you. Proper CI/BI analysis simply has too many steps based on a set of variables that might be hard to script in most instances. One can teach the system to recognize connections and probabilities, but responsible reporting still requires the analyst to fully qualify the information before presenting it. That said, the proper AI implementation gives the analyst a greater scope of insight than she would have from traditional means, and this will lead to more fruitful work product.

Chapter 8:
The next level – auditing your firm's CI and BI

By Dave Whiteside, director of client growth and success at CLIENTSFirst Consulting

Every firm is looking to improve their capabilities around business and competitive intelligence (BCI). The most frequent question I'm asked by far is: "What are other firms doing to improve their BCI?" My typical response is: "Can you first describe where your firm is today so I know what will be of interest to you?" Most people struggle to provide a specific answer of where they are today. What often makes this a difficult question to answer is business and competitive intelligence means different things to different people, even within the same organization. To one, it is a tactical dossier on a target client to prepare for a pitch meeting, providing background on the executives and a general business overview. To another, it's a strategic analysis of how competitors and clients reacted to the firm's recent office opening in a new city. A BCI function in a law firm needs to be able to serve each of these requests as well as many other types of requests from internal clients – usually attorneys.

To serve these internal clients and their various requests for reports and information for BCI, and to continually improve the service level delivered, a firm must regularly address these three key questions:

- Where is our BCI function today?
- Why is our BCI function where it is today?
- How can it be more effective?

The challenge most firms have addressing these questions is they do not have any framework for analyzing exactly what and how they do things today. Instinctively we know when things are not optimized and need change. But what specifically do we change, and why?

One useful method for firms to analyze what they do, how they do it and what needs to be changed is through a lens examining the "people, processes and tools" used to fulfill client needs (Figure 1). A deficiency in any one of the three creates a client service delivery challenge.

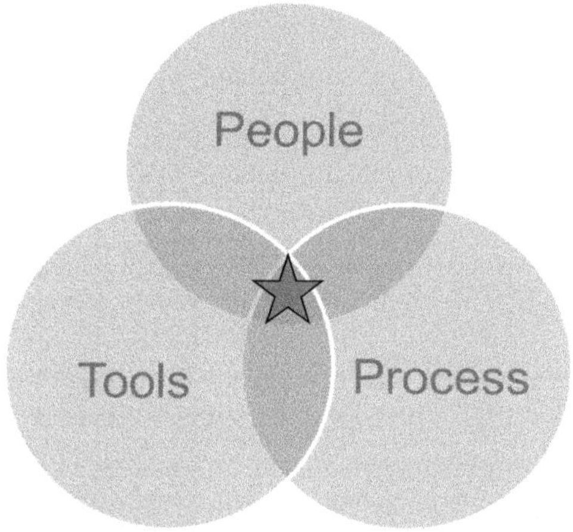

Figure 1: People, Process, Tools: a methodology for client satisfaction

To help identify more specifically map where a firm is today through the people, process and tools lens, this chapter also uses the BCI Capabilities Quadrant (Figure 2) to help identify what the firm needs to change in the people, process and tools equation. Do they have the right tools, and are they leveraging all the tools they have at their disposal most effectively? Do they have the right people and skillsets performing the right work? Do they have the right processes in place to deliver to client requirements?

Assessing BCI maturity using the Capability Quadrant

I often use the Capability Quadrant below to assist firms reviewing where the firm is today. The purpose of the Quadrant is to provide a framework to measure the efficiency and effectiveness of the people, processes and tools and help a firm determine where it lies on the maturity scale. The objective is achieving the ability to deliver BCI that is organizationally efficient and minimize fire drills, while making sure to meet the client's requirements.

The Quadrant helps us identify:

- Do I have the right people/skill mix?
- Are my processes solid, repeatable – or ad hoc?
- Do we have standardized deliverables to meet client needs – to cover 80 percent of all requests?
- Do our toolsets provide data we really need? Are we using all the tools we have available?
- Are users fully trained?
- Do we meet client preferences on formatting – or deliver raw data?
- Do we provide analysis and highlight opportunities and actionable data according to client preference?

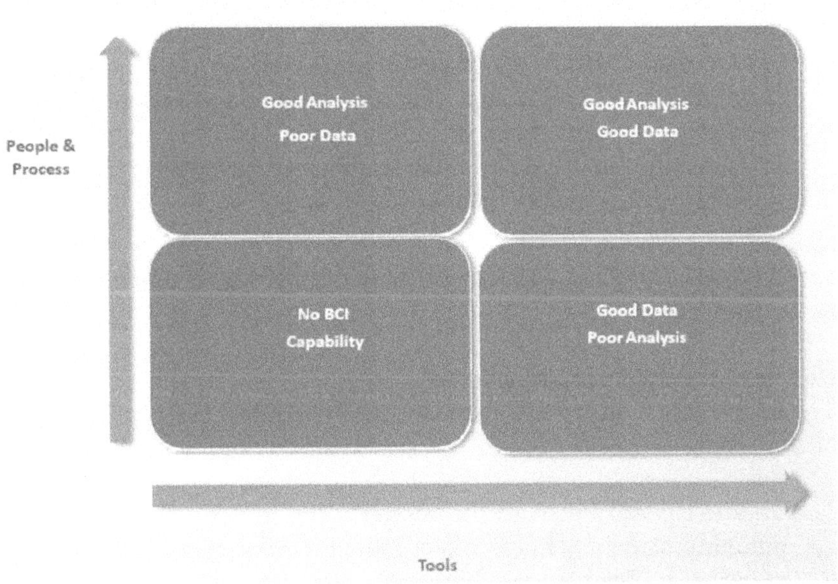

Figure 2: BCI Capabilities Quadrant

Overview of the four sections

- The bottom left is self-explanatory and is usually in firms where the use of BCI is simply not done. Typically seen in small to medium sized firms and where firm culture might not be very collaborative.
- The opposite quadrant (top right) is evident in firms where they have a high-performing and mature BCI function. Things may not be perfectly optimized, but client needs are well met, and the function is seen as helping the firm meet its objectives.

- The top left is not very common. A firm in this quadrant would typically have excellent people skills and defined processes, but they have not invested in acquiring the right toolsets, or possibly leveraging tools that do exist in the firm. Not a common scenario, as usually good people will figure out the tools need to be upgraded. If this scenario does exist, the scenario would typically be good people analyzing poor or incomplete data. Client delivery risks opportunities missed as data was not found or was not current.
- By far the most common scenario is bottom right. Here a firm purchases tools designed to perform a specific function in BCI, but the people assigned to use the tools and analyze the research data do not have the right combination of experience, skills and training to optimally use the tools. Also common in this quadrant are fire-drill type processes; a frequent result is large volumes of data pulled from the purchased tool sets delivered to the client in a voluminous "data dump" that leaves the client frustrated. Staff delivering this data dump are normally not experienced and skilled at leveraging internal tools like the financial system or document management, and data is missed here as well.

Let's look at each of the above as we analyze how we get to the top right of the Quadrant.

Do I have the right people/skill mix?

The people factor on the vertical axis usually requires two or three types of skillsets.

1. The first is attributed to the "miner". The miner can dig up large amounts of data. This is often gained during research or library experience. They are familiar with searching and using the search tools the firm buys, as well as many public domain services available. If the entire BCI process is left up to the "miner", the firm will usually end up in the bottom right of the Quadrant, with the deliverable to the client being excessive amounts of raw data lacking format, organization and any level of opportunity spotting or SWOT analysis (Strengths-Weakness-Opportunities-Threats).
2. The second needed for success is the "analyzer". This is often a business development team member who communicates directly to the client, or in some cases is the client. This skillset analyses and

synthesizes large amounts of raw data into a concise and actionable deliverable. They are often skilled at opportunity spotting and SWOT type analysis. If the entire process is left to the analyzer, the deliverable is typically much more concise, and some opportunities likely identified. The risk is that this skill often isn't capable of thoroughly searching many of the tools; this means that important information – and thus opportunities – may not be discovered.

3. The third skillset is less common in firms, but is growing in popularity every day: the quantitative analyst, or the "quants". The quants specializes in the application of mathematical and statistical methods, such as numerical or quantitative techniques. This skillset is very adept at taking BCI data and finding the key data points – for example, looking at the balance sheet of a target or prospect to see where opportunities or issues may lie. They often can also look at the firm's internal numbers around staffing ratios, rates and other data that can be highly useful in a pitch or proposal. I have never seen a firm where the BCI function falls to this skillset alone. However, if your BCI team does not have a full-time quant, make a friend and adjunct them to your team. They often spot trends and data points other people do not see.

From a staffing perspective, it is very difficult to find highly proficient levels of these skills. These people tend to be concentrated in large firms. Finding a single person with two of the three skills, let alone all three skills, is tough. In firms fortunate enough to staff specialists in all these roles, the key is getting them operating as an effective team. Doing so will elevate the BCI function to either the top left or top right of the Quadrant. For smaller firms, the challenge is that there is not enough demand to justify hiring all these skillsets, so they need to try and find the right skill mix in possibly just one resource. There are certainly generalists in firms who have some level of proficiency with two or even all three skills, but finding one person highly skilled in even two is difficult. Firms might consider outside consultants to fill this lack on an as needed basis.

Do I have the tools and know how to use them?

The tools factor on the horizontal axis is a combination of what we have and the questions of whether we know how to best utilize them. Tools fall into two categories: internal and external. Let's look at each and how they can be used for BCI.

Internal marketing tools

Firms have internal tools for marketing and business development purposes. A website is a staple in every firm and the core function is to display content, with the most frequently visited pages typically being attorney bios and experience, where prospects are credentialing a lawyer. Customer relationship management/enterprise relationship management (CRM/ERM) systems are common in many. An "experience database" is not as common but very useful, with the primary function of taking internal matter data and translating internal data to market-facing data. CRM/ERM systems are designed to collect data about clients and prospects and provide a historical view of who we know, who knows them the best, and ideally what interactions we have had with them as far as meetings, events attended, newsletters subscribed to, social media interaction and other data. The goal is to understand their "engagement level" with us – both past and present – and make it available to include in a BCI report if appropriate. Key data that can be mined from these tools includes:

- Who knows who – which attorneys have relationships with which clients/prospects (ERM/CRM)?
- What interactions do we currently have with them (newsletters, blogs, Twitter or other feeds subscribed to or future events signed up for [CRM/website])?
- Past interactions – what did they attend and subscribe to in past (CRM/website)?
- What work have we performed successfully for them (time and billing system or experience system)?
- Client or prospect preferences – do they prefer email or phone? Who is their assistant? Spouse? Children? Favorite teams? Dietary restrictions? Civic involvement? Religion? Politics? School/alumni? Law firm employment? This information would ideally be in the CRM, but it's likely you'll need to look in several places.

External tools

Company websites, LinkedIn, Facebook, Twitter and other social media are usually free and can provide a wealth of information on a prospect. D&B Hoovers, Monitor Suite, Capital IQ, Pitchbook, Bloomberg, The Deal, Westlaw, Ibis World, Lexis or other external subscription information tools provide targeted help with business and legal history if available. These are subscription-based and as a rule rely on publicly available information through filings and news. They are often much easier to use than internal systems, as they are designed to pull together information in a more consumable format. Key data that can be mined from these tools includes:

- Company website – for larger companies this is a treasure trove, with everything from officers' and directors' bios to SEC filings, business organization and structure, and business strategy and direction;
- LinkedIn, Facebook – this helps you ascertain background and relationships in common;
- Hoovers – Hoovers provides a business overview of a company as well as allowing for list-building based on business criteria like size, sales volume, industry, and location;
- Monitor Suite – This tool from Thomson Reuters provides information on three main areas: litigation, deals and intellectual property. There are many uses for this tool; it has capabilities for list-building and other handy functions, but the most common use is to run reports on companies, industries, law firms and lawyers. A report on a company, for example, can show which law firms/lawyers are hired for litigation, IP or deal work. Frequency work occurs, jurisdictions/geography, opposing counsel, and more;
- Pitch Book, Capital IQ, The Deal, Bloomberg, and Thomson Reuters Eikon are all tools that are used for doing "deal" work. Deal work broadly might include M&A, private equity, bond work and more, with information on parties, representation and more;
- Legal research with Westlaw & Lexis – these two tools are best known for their "legal research". The ability to find cases and statutes "on point" is the traditional use case, but both are adding more databases and tools that not only facilitate but target business developers; and
- Industry research is an area that gets a lot of discussion. Google is certainly the most widely used and will find a large mass of information. The time required is the biggest challenge relating to Google and other wide search tools. Ibis World has a very straight forward industry research tool that breaks down industries and major players. Gartner, Forrester and others have tools that rate companies and products, with some free but most behind

a subscription wall. One of the most valuable reasons to search industry information is to compare a single company against their peers. Do their legal issues, for example, trend with peer companies?

Do we have our BCI processes optimized?

The processes factor is on the vertical axis with the people. The two are highly intertwined and is likely the origin of the phrase: "The process worked perfectly until we added in the people." The biggest challenge of process change is almost always the people. Ask the question: "Will instituting new processes require changes to behaviors to be sure we are not simply plugging old fixtures into new plumbing?"

No two firms have – nor need to have – identical processes. However, firms which demonstrate success absolutely have defined processes. Here are some common examples of processes used:

- Role identification – who does what? Who is the researcher? The analyzer? Clearly define the handoff point;
- Track the lifecycle of every report – when did it come in and go out? Who did what on a report? Who does a follow-up to be sure the client is satisfied?
- Client processes – defined processes around how clients request BCI reports and clear expectations around what will be delivered and expected delivery time;
- Communication planning – to message out what is available to the client. I have worked with firms to create report examples, print out copies and put them in notebook with a table of contents, bring all clients in for a breakfast or lunch, and walk them through what is available and the process to request one. Include description of each report type and expectations around delivery times;
- Provide training on what is delivered in the report and don't assume the client will figure it out on their own;
- Create expectations with clients as far as what BCI is and how complete a report they can or should expect. Strive to perfection but adhere to the BCI rule of 80 percent (when 80 percent is certain, go with it, as perfection is usually not attainable);
- Get client feedback. What was useful and what was not? You have to ask, as rarely do attorneys give feedback without prompting, unless it was really bad;

- Track "wins and losses" for reports. No attorney ever comes back from a pitch meeting shouting out how the BCI report used to prep for the meeting created the win, but keep these stats for leadership reports. Many firms also track what resources might have been needed to better or more completely satisfy a client request if there were challenges – for example, we did not have the right tools / data to identify the target companies M&A work history;
- Build BCI use into attorney coaching programs. If your firm uses external coaches, ask them if they incorporate BCI information into their coaching methods. How can the internal team support that need? If you use internal coaching resources, build BCI information into the coaching for targeting and pitch preparation; and
- Look for other opportunities to leverage BCI. Is your managing partner headed to client interviews? Firm retreat coming up, or industry team meetings?

The quest for improvement of BCI in firms is ongoing and can never be 100 percent achieved. However, continual review of client needs, ongoing investment in people and their training, having the right toolset to support the business requirements of the clients, and a focus on ongoing process improvement will create an environment for BCI success in any firm.

Chapter 9: Matter experience – the centerpiece of your business development strategy

By Keith N Wewe, VP of strategy and solutions at Content Pilot LLC

Matter experience inside the law firm is unarguably the most informative business intelligence that should be gathered to support the sales function. However, it's an area where many firms continue to fail because they neither have a solid process in place for collecting the data and knowing what to do with it once it's there, nor are they employing effective techniques in determining which matter experience most aligns with client needs.

The groundbreaking firms who saw matter experience early on as their most important sales tool attempted to gain a deeper understanding of this information by reviewing data housed in their time and billing systems. This gave them insight into what type of work the firm was doing, who they were doing it for, and who was working on it. And while this data was great at giving lawyers a quick list of matter experience about which to boast, lawyers quickly determined that this information did not tell the story of the matter in a way that was meaningful to potential clients. It was missing the deeper data and robust descriptions around the nuances of the matter for firms to really know if, and how, it aligned with specific client needs.

Imagine the difference between searching M&A-specific matters by billing lawyers, rates and hours worked and searching the same matter experience by the role of the firm or client; the name, industry, public status and financial advisors to the acquiror, seller or target; and whether alternative fee arrangements were offered to the client. The ability to drill down into the specifics of a matter is invaluable intellectual capital that was not being captured.

To solve this problem, firms have started to look to either their internal technology teams or third-party providers to build business intelligence technologies to facilitate the capture of this information. These systems integrate with time and billing, matter intake, human resource and pricing analytics technology platforms across the firm to aggregate information about the matter into a single repository. And once there, human assets would take over and supplement it with additional data that could only be provided by someone familiar with the matter.

When implemented based on the unique needs of each firm, these tools allow law firms to search their extensive databases on all their matter experience based on subtle differences important to individual clients and package it in marketing materials for quick delivery. And "when handled and analyzed with intent, the data resulting from a business's daily operations and can be revelatory" and allow these "sophisticated firms [to gain] an edge over the competition by utilizing data to support better decision-making in both the practice and business of law."[1]

However, these business intelligence technologies are only one part of the equation because, by nature, they are only able to tell the story of the firm – a story that is based on looking backwards and not forwards. For firms looking to align their story with that of their clients, they need a deeper understanding of client need. This is where business intelligence and competitive intelligence intersect with matter experience serving as the centerpiece for your business development strategy.

How does competitive intelligence fit in?

The competitive intelligence discipline inside the law firms continues to advance at high rates,[2] which spells good news for the legal industry and associated sales efforts. From a human resource perspective, dedicated CI employees are working to provide lawyers with information on their current and potential clients so they can make insightful decisions on sales initiatives. And technology firms are creating better, faster and more products to support the function of their human counterparts.

This is what the process mostly looks like now.

A current or potential client has a matter for which they want to hire outside counsel. That matter can be presented to the firm via the request for proposal process or perhaps over a lunch meeting with no real competitive component. Regardless of how the firm came to know about the matter, they are now in a position to convince the client that they are better suited to handle the matter than the law firm across the street. To do that, they need to craft a story that demonstrates their expertise in that area of law by relying on the best business intelligence they have – their matter experience. But which specific matter experience should the firm offer? If the firm is capturing all their matter experience, they will have thousands of matters that align with the client's need – although the "spaghetti against the wall approach" of offering thousands of matters as an example of expertise is ineffective. To prove relevance and win the work, firms must offer the ten to twelve pieces of matter experience that best align with the client's need.

To help make that determination, CI staff carefully study the client by learning about their current legal staff and their related expertise, gathering applicable news articles around the need, studying their contacts with key employees who work with the client company, and studying any work the firm has done for the client in the past and how well it was performed. Once the data is in hand, the matter experience of the firm is chosen based how it aligns not only with the stated need, but with the overall clients' strategy and skills of the individual lawyers employed by the client.

Sounds straightforward, right? However, is this competitive intelligence information providing firms with better results and more wins? Is there better information that CI professionals should be gathering? What proactive activities should CI departments be doing around client need, instead of the reactive response required when a potential client initiates a request?

A study on the topic published by Acritas showed that only eight percent of respondents consider their CI function to be highly effective in helping the firm make better, more informed decisions.[3] This lack of effectiveness is attributable to other pieces of information in the study that showed 70 percent of survey respondents defined CI as providing a "better understanding [of] clients and prospects," while 47 percent of respondents defined it as researching the market and client penetration of "peer firms/competitive analysis." An even lower number of respondents – eight percent – defined CI as providing "peer firm/competitor analysis" in operational and financial dealings.

Of course, client and prospect information is highly informative data and another necessary part of the equation of placing matter experience at the center of your business development strategy. It appears from the Acritas study, therefore, that firms are getting this right. However, the study also indicates that most firms, when considering their key competitors, aren't exercising the same CI process they are employing when researching their prospective clients. This is a missed opportunity and where firms are getting it wrong.

Every law firm in the world competes for business. And while there remains a general feeling in the legal industry that, apart from the most elite law firms like Cravath, Wachtell, Skadden, and others,[4] law firms are a homogenous group of businesses with the same experience, doing the same work for the same clients, the legal industry is changing. It's transitioning to a marketplace where "legal consumers – not 'smart lawyers' – are now calling the shots," where "consumers demand more choice, transparency, competition, price predictability, and direct access to providers."[5]

With this change afoot in the marketplace, it's essential for law firms to utilize CI departments to determine who their competitors are in their key markets, practice areas, industries and sectors – and understand their strengths and weaknesses just as they would work to understand their own. They need to ask, in their matter pursuits, against whom they are competing, so that business intelligence may also be provided based on the other smart lawyers in the room.

As we pondered about business intelligence data earlier, imagine the difference between searching M&A-specific matters by the bench strength of the client, their annual legal spend, and primary and secondary locations and searching the same matter experience by the bench strength of your key competitors; the number of partners, counsel and associates in key geographic markets; the number of other M&A deals they have completed in the past two years; the complexity, amount and "star power" of the deals they have completed; and their fee structure and use of alternative fee arrangements when working with their clients.

It's essential in a buyers' market that we meet the demands of choice, transparency, competition and price predictability to clearly delineate with your matter experience how you are different from others. Competitive intelligence, completed properly, will help achieve this.

Of interest in the study is that "80 percent of law firms' CI departments are more reactive than proactive, while 61 percent of respondents indicated that they are more tactical than strategic." These two statistics are related, as the failure of CI departments to spend time proactively providing market insight is directly proportional to their inability to spend the time needed to create law firm strategy – they are too busy rushing from request-to-request and project-to-project to provide lawyers information they are requesting.

Again, imagine the difference between searching M&A-specific matters by the reactive needs brought to you by your clients and prospects and searching the same matter experience by what is predicted to happen with M&A five years down the road. And furthering that idea to build law firm expertise in areas where the market is headed, as opposed to spending time and resources to create practice expertise in a reactionary manner.

As with business intelligence, these unique competitive strategies are still only another part of the equation. Together, they offer the ability to align your best matter experience with the needs of your clients, their business, your competitors, and the future of the industry. However, these remain decisions that require human intervention and require time, resources and money from teams already stretched too thin. For firms looking to use a deeper level of analytical data in determining which matter experience best resonates with potential clients, they must rely on data about how potential client view your matter experience in their buying decisions. This is where business intelligence and competitive intelligence intersect with artificial intelligence.

Where does artificial intelligence play a role?

In a world where computers are creating generated images of human beings that are impossible to distinguish from the real images themselves,[6] using a computer to surface the matter experience that best aligns with client need doesn't require much stretch of the imagination.

Consider the four following opportunities where a machine can learn how potential clients are using your matter experience in making a buying decision:

1. Creating technologies that allow firms to categorize how often a piece of experience is included in pitch and proposals;
2. Categorizing which matter experience – per market, practice area, industry and sectors – leads to the wins – big and small;
3. Noting how often website visitors are reviewing specific pieces of experience on your website and where they go from there; and
4. Feeding competitive intelligence attributes of your potential clients and competitors and allowing technology to surface the matter experience best aligned based on all the factors presented.

This type of big data is necessary because the human behavior of your potential clients and how they are interacting with your experience is essential in understanding their buying trends related to your best business intelligence.

However, artificial intelligence in legal isn't without its challenges. For machine learning to take hold, technology platforms inside law firms require thousands of learning sets before the system can surface actionable matters, which means these systems require real and sustained adoption by lawyers and business development professionals. To achieve this, a strong process must be adopted.

For many firms, process is synonymous with removing barriers and changing bad habits and replacing them with good habits that support your end goal, which can be challenging in firms where culture runs deep. Process also isn't a "one-size-fits-all" approach. What works for one firm may not work for another, so these processes must be tailored to the specific human employees and technology assets in place.

Where do we go from here?

From here, we need to get busy creating strategies and processes that pull matter experience out of the dark ages and into the technology-driven world. Law firms have a real opportunity to use their matter experience as an asset, differentiator and tool to increase wins at their firms.

And time is of the essence. As Jordan Furlong notes, "'The future' is an anesthetic. It will lull you to sleep if you let it. Wake up to the challenges, the crises and the rare opportunities that are being presented to you today, right now, in this moment. There is no future. There's only right now. Get up, right now, and do something about it."[7]

References

1. Data and Analytics: Transforming Law Firms, ALM Intelligence and Lexis Nexis, January 2019, https://www.law.com/2019/01/17/data-analytics-transforming-law-firms/
2. The Maturation of Competitive Intelligence in Law Firms, Rod Osborne, August 15, 2016, https://www.mlaglobal.com/en/knowledge-library/articles/the-maturation-of-competitive-intelligence-in-law-firms?byconsultantorauthor=rod-osborne
3. The Evolution of Competitive Intelligence in Law Firms, Acritas, https://www.acritas.com/competitive-intelligence-report
4. Vault's Top 100 Law Firms For 2019, Vault, June 20, 2018, http://www.vault.com/blog/vaults-law-blog-legal-careers-and-industry-news/vaults-top-100-law-firms-for-2019/
5. Differentiation in the New Legal Marketplace and Why It Matters, Mark Cohen, Forbes, January 2, 2018, https://www.forbes.com/sites/markcohen1/2018/01/02/differentiation-in-the-new-legal-marketplace-and-why-it-matters/#208aa56738ef
6. Look at These Incredibly Realistic Faces Generated by a Neural Network. None of these people are real, Victor Tangermann, December 13, 2018, https://futurism.com/incredibly-realistic-faces-generated-neural-network
7. Smartlaw 2.0: Expert insights for the future of law, HighQ and Jordan Furlong.

www.ingramcontent.com/pod-product-compliance
Ingram Content Group UK Ltd.
Pitfield, Milton Keynes, MK11 3LW, UK
UKHW021834131026
9310IPUK00004B/77

9 781783 583683